THE
PILLARED
CITY

THE PILLARED CITY

Greek Revival Mobile

JOHN S. SLEDGE

Mobile Historic Development Commission

Photography by SHEILA HAGLER

THE UNIVERSITY OF GEORGIA PRESS

Athens & London

Published through the generosity of The A. S. Mitchell Foundation *Mobile, Alabama*

© 2009 by the
University of Georgia Press
Athens, Georgia 30602
www.ugapress.org
Photography © 2009 by Sheila Hagler
All rights reserved
Designed by Richard Hendel
Set in Monticello and Didot types by
April Leidig-Higgins, Copperline Book Services
Printed and bound by Kings Time Printing
The paper in this book meets the guidelines for
permanence and durability of the Committee on
Production Guidelines for Book Longevity of the
Council on Library Resources.

Printed in China

13 12 11 10 09 C 5 4 3 2 1

Library of Congress Cataloging-in-Publication Data
Sledge, John S. (John Sturdivant), 1957–
 The pillared city : Greek revival Mobile / John S. Sledge ;
photography by Sheila Hagler.
  p. cm.
Includes bibliographical references and index.
ISBN-13: 978-0-8203-3020-4 (cloth : alk. paper)
ISBN-10: 0-8203-3020-5 (cloth : alk. paper)
 1. Greek revival (Architecture) — Alabama — Mobile.
2. Mobile (Ala.) — Buildings, structures, etc. I. Hagler,
Sheila. II. Title.
NA735.M62S59 2009
724'.230976122 — dc22
                                                    2008050098

British Library Cataloging-in-Publication Data available

*This one's for Lynn,
my beautiful wife*

CONTENTS

PREFACE:

My Georgia Cottage ix

Acknowledgments xvii

Photographer's Note xxi

INTRODUCTION:

Greek Revival Architecture in America 1

CHAPTER 1.

Pillared Beginnings in Antebellum Mobile 25

CHAPTER 2.

Pillared City, Pillared Ruin, 1836–1839 47

CHAPTER 3.

Town and Country Classicism, 1840–1865 82

EPILOGUE:

The Long Reverberation 115

List of Abbreviations 125

Notes 127

Glossary 137

Bibliography 141

Index 145

Georgia Cottage, 2008. This Spring Hill Avenue landmark has long arrested passersby. Other than minor interior modifications, it stands substantially as built more than 160 years ago.

PREFACE

MY GEORGIA COTTAGE

It stands graceful, elegant, and serene at the end of a moss-draped oak allée down in old Mobile. Georgia Cottage, so named for its original owner's Peach State roots, was my childhood Arcadia, an enchanted world where past and present seamlessly merged. As I explored its exotic rooms and grounds, and pondered its many intriguing mysteries, I came to acquire a profound appreciation for historic architecture, landscape, art, antiques, family, and memory. It was there, at a very young age indeed, that I became a historian. In retrospect, I could hardly have become anything else.

It was an aesthetic education to live within those walls.
—*Charles Ryder in Evelyn Waugh's Brideshead Revisited*

Georgia Cottage was built around 1845 — the records don't provide a precise date — by a pair of newlyweds hopefully embarked upon their future. Mary J. Delbarco, the granddaughter of a Georgia pioneer, was given a nine-acre share of an old Spanish land grant located along the north side of the Spring Hill Road in 1837. Shortly thereafter she married a Virginia-born cotton factor (a middleman who brokered cotton sales) named William A. Hardaway. Family legend holds that the home's heavy cypress timbers were hewn out and pegged together by slave labor. It's certainly a possibility — the Hardaways owned a dozen human beings at the time, valued at four thousand dollars — but there is no way to definitively document whether or not these individuals contributed to the construction.[1]

Nor, as is typical with so many antebellum homes, is there any record of exactly who was responsible for Georgia Cottage's design. It could have been a talented local architect, or an itinerant one with a pattern book and ambition, or any one of a dozen capable craftsmen then working in Alabama's seaport. The Hardaways probably had a hand in it as well, influenced by other homes they might have seen and admired around the South. Whoever was responsible, his genius is readily apparent. In form, plan, and overall tone, Georgia Cottage exhibits an admirable simplicity. But to call it plain would be a mistake. It is, in fact, beautifully integrated with its setting and perfectly fits the popular conception of an old southern home. Its architecture represents a masterful blending of formal and informal elements — a Greek Revival vocabulary mellowed and sweetened by the Deep South vernacular. Boxed columns support the wide verandah as well as the wing porches, which invite repose and reflection in the Alabama heat. In imitation of the old Greek temples, the facade is smoothly plastered with a concoction of crushed oyster shells, pig bristles, lime, and sand, whereas the sides and rear of the home are covered in painted wooden siding. The low-slung hip roof is gently framed, or more properly, embowered, by overarching live oak limbs.

The interior plan, little altered since construction, consists of a wide central hallway with double parlors to either side, a tiny rear kitchen with enclosed back porch, and a pair of matching side wings that each hold a small bedroom and bath. The interior trim — door, window frames, and mantels — presents a subtle play of well-proportioned order and symmetry amid generous space. The wide hall and airy high-ceilinged rooms allow cooling zephyrs to circulate freely, and the front parlors feature jibbed windows, so named for the little paneled doors positioned below the sash, enabling each window to be thrown open and converted into an extra doorway onto the verandah whenever mood or necessity dictates. Finer touches appear here and there — polished slate hearths, silver-plated doorknobs and keyhole covers, lovely plaster crown molding, and simple concentric medallions on the hall and parlor ceilings.

Unfortunately for the Hardaways, they were unable to hold the house for long and in 1857 sold it to the woman who would become its most famous resident. (Actually, they sold it to the woman's father, but she was the moneyed party.) Augusta Jane Evans was a twenty-two-year-old Georgian with one novel under her belt, *Inez: A Tale of the Alamo* (1855) (an anti-Catholic diatribe inspired by a short sojourn in San Antonio), and enough royalties in her pocket to set the family up in the grand new lodgings. She lived there until her marriage in 1868 and penned several other novels in her bedroom wing, including *Beulah* (1859), *Macaria* (1864), and the wildly popular *St. Elmo* (1866). She was the first American female author to make over $100,000 from her writings. That Georgia Cottage was the perfect retreat is reflected in Evans's warm references to it in her letters. On November 15, 1860, for example, she described it as "my dear quiet country sanctum-Sanctorum, my Mecca of rest."[2]

There were a handful of other owners down the decades until my grandfather, Edward Simmons Sledge, a physician, and my grandmother, Mary Frank Sturdivant Sledge, purchased the property in 1935. My grandmother immediately took to the house and loved it heart and soul. She was among the first owners of historic homes in Mobile to open her doors to tours, allowing strangers to traipse through the interior. My father often chuckled at the memory of the fantastic tales she would tell the gawking tourists.[3]

My own connection to Georgia Cottage and the fascinating city where it was built thus dates back to my infancy, more than half a century. My parents met

Georgia Cottage, ca. 1960, as it was during my childhood. The aspidistras, planted in 1950, remain healthy to this day, though the Spanish moss has been greatly diminished by air pollution. The driveway was poorly covered by shredded asphalt roofing, which my grandmother soon replaced, much to my disappointment, with the harder-to-run-on pea gravel. (Author's collection.)

and married in Mobile, and though they raised me in Florida and central Alabama, our frequent trips to the Port City and warm family relations made it feel more like home than the hardscrabble landscape around Birmingham. Even as a small child, I was attuned to the differences as we hurtled toward the coast — a swampier, brooding landscape; a tang of sea salt; and the paper mills' sulfurous breath in the softening air. And when we finally turned onto Spring Hill Avenue, the stately live oaks festooned with moss and the grand, columned homes left no doubt that we were back. To my impressionable mind, Mobile loomed large as a place where there was more history, and the people, living and dead, were more colorful than upstate.

At the center of it all was Georgia Cottage. I will never forget the thrill when we arrived after so many tiring hours on the road. We were greeted from the verandah by my grandmother's unmistakable halloo (she amplified the pitch on the last syllable of my mother's name, "Jean-IE!"), and after much fuss we were ushered into a magical realm. This was where my father had spent his adolescence, and the relics of those years were still manifest — in the back room where he slept, an old hunting rifle, and most exciting of all, in the basement (a coastal rarity), a collection of Civil War cannonballs he had dug up at Spanish Fort over the bay, the site of one of the doleful conflict's last big battles.

If I close my eyes, I can still picture it all and even conjure the rich smells that

(Opposite) The Georgia Cottage dining room as viewed from the front parlor, 1964. This image was taken for an article in Antiques *magazine, and the photographer's reflection can be seen in the mirror atop the Hepplewhite sideboard. The Oriental rug in the foreground was from a palace in Constantinople, which my grandfather bought at the estate sale of a St. Louis editor. Nothing in Georgia Cottage was ordinary, and everything had a story. (Courtesy of Thigpen Photography.)*

first greeted my nostrils when I tumbled out of the car — a vague, not unpleasant, earthy mélange of vegetative decay, tea olive, and magnolia blossoms, and once inside the house, cloves, mothballs, and the spicy hint of shrimp gumbo.

My grandmother's exquisite taste and love for art and antiques made the interior a veritable museum. The hallway displayed a colorful Shiraz rug, and the west wall was dominated by a large oil painting in a gilded frame titled *Henrietta at the Well*. Like everything else in Georgia Cottage, the picture had a distinguished pedigree, having originally hung in the old Emanuel House, one of Mobile's most sophisticated Greek Revival town homes, designed by New York architects James and Charles Dakin and James Gallier and, sadly, demolished in 1936, only a year after my grandparents bought Georgia Cottage.

The rooms on the hallway's east side were the most impressive in the house. They are still divided by a large set of heavy pocket doors set in a lovely eared architrave surround and running on a metal track (or "way" as Minard Lafever described this kind of device in his seminal 1835 pattern book *The Beauties of Modern Architecture*). I spent many happy hours arranging my toy Civil War soldiers along this way, which nicely doubled as a railroad track. Through languid afternoons my troops would battle across the hardwood floors, the South always victorious.

My grandmother used the front east room as a formal parlor and had furnished it with mid-nineteenth-century French rosewood pieces and a marble-top table that had once belonged to Jefferson Davis. The north wall was hung with several Taj Mahal monotypes by the Scottish painter Roderick MacKenzie, whom my grandmother had befriended during his difficult final years in Mobile. This room was especially significant because Augusta Jane Evans married Colonel Lorenzo Wilson here, clad, so the story goes, in deep mourning for her years-dead father. That's the kind of woman she was.

The room behind the parlor served as the dining room and was separated from the small kitchen behind it by a paneled door on spring hinges that creaked rustily every time my grandmother's wonderful cook, Ida, pushed it open. The dining room included a West Indian linen press with a ghastly death mask of Shakespeare atop, a Hepplewhite sideboard with large glass hurricane shades, and a Tiffany coffee service. Meals were served on an Empire table surrounded by eight Chippendale chairs. Over the mantel on the east wall was a primitive American painting that had come to early nineteenth-century Alabama from New Hampshire via wagon, and on the west wall was another MacKenzie, this one a softly glowing pastel of Georgia Cottage.

The rooms to the west of the hallway included my grandmother's bedroom at the front and a guest bedroom to the rear, with a small bathroom between. Gran slept in a magnificent tester bed that she was told had originally belonged to the

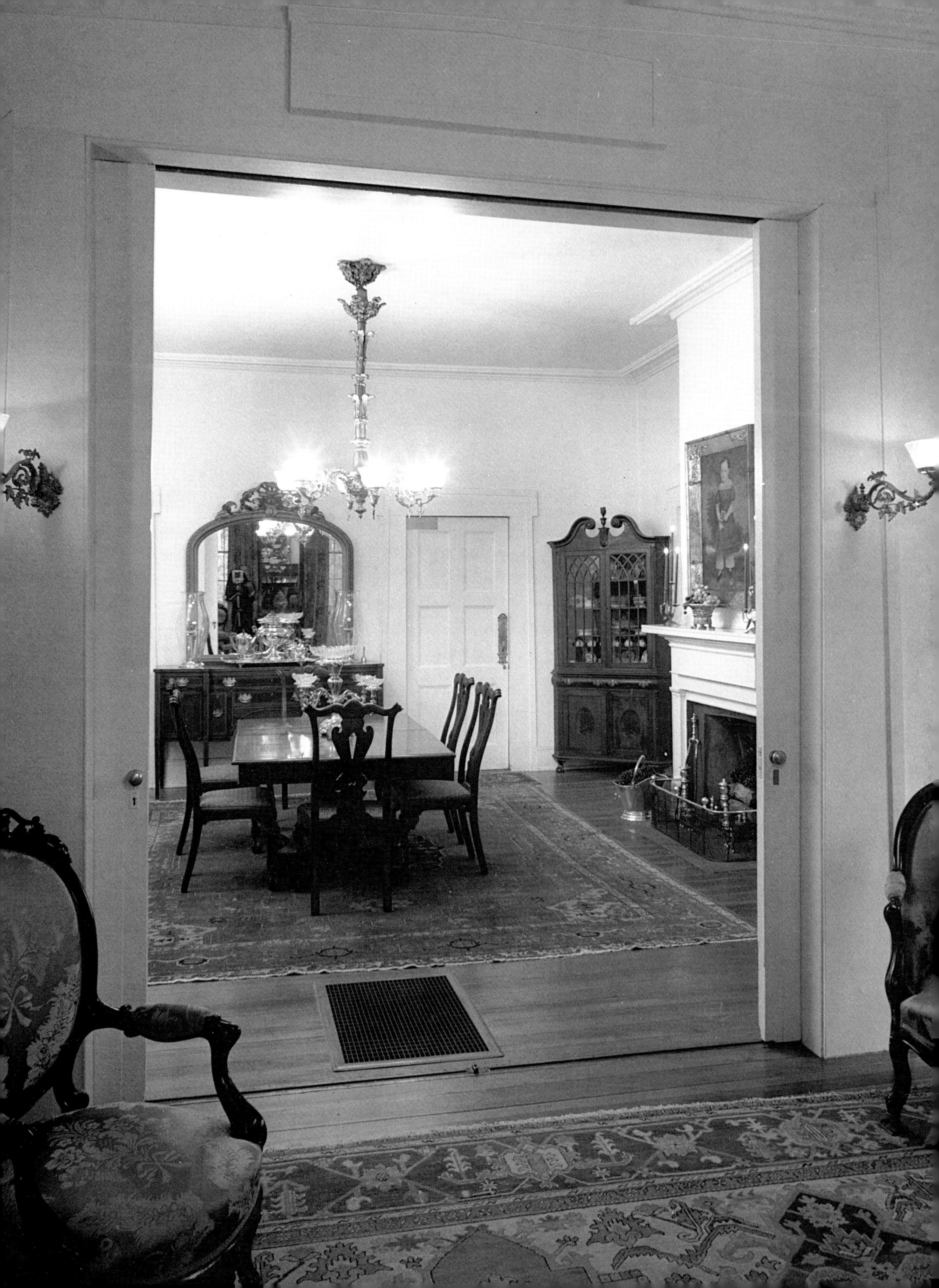

English essayist Charles Lamb and been brought to New Orleans by a descendent. As Gran later recalled, "It took me ten years and five trips before I could get it in 1943."[4] With its elaborate headboard, canopy, and silk comforter, it sheltered her dreams for decades. This room was also my favorite winter retreat. I spent many contented hours ensconced before a sputtering coal fire, reading about ancient Greece and Rome, little guessing the distant echoes between those worlds and the place where I sat.

On our family visits, I slept in the rear guest bedroom, which had been my father's quarters. The setting was much simpler here, with a small sleigh bed that had belonged to my great-grandmother. Tempered by poverty during Reconstruction, she was a practical and unpretentious woman who had served as dean of women at Huntingdon College in Montgomery. This room's standout item of interest, though, was not a piece of furniture or art but rather a bubbled and wavy windowpane that had the names of the original owners and their children cut into the glass, probably with a diamond ring.

The back porch was another favorite spot. Here I could indulge my boyish rambunctiousness without fear of reprisal, running from one end to the other and then rocking furiously in an old cowhide rocker given to my grandfather by a grateful patient during the Depression. Nor will I forget the wild excitement that chilly fall morning when my pajama-clad father chased a monster ship rat around the porch with an old broom; this was high drama of the best sort, and I jumped up and down, shouting encouragement. The back porch was also where the heavy trapdoor with its iron ring led down into the musty wine cellar. I loved to lift it up and push it back against the kitchen wall, and then descend, feeling the temperature drop as I got below floor level. Supposedly, when the former Confederate politico and general Robert Toombs fled for Cuba, Augusta Jane bundled him down these very steps, though whether to hide him from disgusted Southerners or vengeful Yankees I never knew. Rough wooden shelves stood in the middle of the space, and the air was permeated with the smell of sandy loam, cork, and crockery. This was where the cannonballs were, including an intact round of grapeshot, still securely bound with iron rings and looking every bit as menacing as it no doubt did in 1865.

When I tired of the house itself, the grounds beckoned with their own myriad wonders. The long allée, lined by live oaks, aspidistras (or "cast iron," as it's popularly called), azaleas, and four varieties of camellias, provided a spectacular stage for games of hide-and-go-seek with my younger cousin Mary Louise, and the concrete goldfish pond just in front of the house yielded endless diversion around its chipped, mossy rim.

In the spring of 1968, Mary Louise and I were dragged from our gambols and put into our Sunday best to unveil a large historic marker out on Spring Hill

Avenue designating Georgia Cottage as the home of Augusta Evans Wilson. No sooner had we yanked the cloth from the marker and done homage to Miss 'Gusta than we were off down the driveway again, pursuing our endless games and rambles.

It all seems so long ago now. My grandmother sold the house to Augustine Meaher III in 1976 and moved into the historic St. Charles Apartments on Government Street. I visited her frequently there as a college student, and with many of the same furnishings and smells, her apartment was a powerful reminder of Georgia Cottage. But, though I realized it only much later, the old times were irretrievably lost. Never again would I have such a splendidly appointed playground. Georgia Cottage can still exert its power over me, though. Even now, thirty years beyond its sale and twenty years beyond Gran's death, whenever I drive out Spring Hill Avenue and glimpse that columned verandah down the long allée, I feel a clutch of the heart. There, more than anywhere else for me, is Mobile.

Detail, Hall-Ford House facade. The fluted pilaster clearly denotes the strong classical influence on this early nineteenth-century cottage.

ACKNOWLEDGMENTS

This book completes the Old Mobile trilogy that Sheila Hagler and I began a decade ago. Taken collectively, *Cities of Silence: A Guide to Mobile's Historic Cemeteries*, *An Ornament to the City: Old Mobile Ironwork*, and now *The Pillared City: Greek Revival Mobile* represent a celebration of the priceless historic legacies of the city we hold dear. Each of these books also goes to the heart of our conviction that any profound understanding of Mobile must begin with its rich and colorful past.

The incredible A. S. Mitchell Foundation has supported this endeavor from the beginning, and I am greatly indebted to its visionary trustees — Joseph Meaher, Augustine Meaher III, David Dukes, Judge Brevard Hand, Frank Vinson, and Kenneth Vinson. I must single out Joseph Meaher for his receptivity to projects like this in the idea phase and invaluable help in presenting them to the trustees in a positive light. Augustine Meaher III and his wife Mary Lou deserve additional praise for their loving stewardship of my grandmother's old home, Georgia Cottage. The house always looks great, and they are unfailingly generous in opening it up to me whenever I ask.

I cannot overemphasize the importance of the City of Mobile's support in writing this book. It simply would not have been possible otherwise. From the top down, everyone has been fantastic. To begin with, Mayor Sam Jones and Executive Director of Cultural and Civic Development Robert O. Bostwick Jr. have shown that they care immeasurably about the city's historic resources and believe that books are a useful way to spread knowledge and pride. To that end, Devereaux Bemis, director of the Mobile Historic Development Commission, graciously allowed me the office time to research and write. Amid the pressures and emergencies of the moment, he never wavered from that position. My colleagues Anne Crutcher (now retired), Aileen de la Torre (now moved on), Kathleen Padgett (also moved on), Keri Coumanis, Sandra Franks, and Shaun Wilson were unfailingly patient with my bleary-eyed distraction during this project, and for that I am grateful.

Numerous institutions and individuals helped along the way. At the Mobile Municipal Archives, Edward (Ned) Harkins, Pamela Major, Rosella Coker, Susan Pate, and Zennia Calhoun were of invaluable assistance. Others include

Sheryl Somathilake, Amy Beach, and Jane Daugherty at the Local History and Genealogy Branch of the Mobile Public Library; David Alsobrook, Sheila Flanagan, Charles Torrey, Lonnie Adams, Ellie Skinner, Martha Otts, Jacob Laurence, and Todd Kreamer at the Museum of Mobile; Johnny Cook (dean of the cathedral) and Victor Stanton (archivist) at Christ Episcopal Church; Carol Ellis, Barbara Asmus, and Scotty Kirkland at the University of South Alabama Archives; Marilyn Culpepper and Christine Cramer at the Historic Mobile Preservation Society; Claire Lewis Evans at the University of Alabama Press; Charles Boyle and Alicia Parker at the Spring Hill College Archives; Laura Seymour and Bobby Purifoy at the Government Street Presbyterian Church; and Dr. Harold Dodge, former school superintendent at Barton Academy, as well as Nancy Pierce and Acie Hall. Tom Lanham at the Louisiana State Museum was helpful, as were Irene Wainwright at the New Orleans Public Library and the wonderful staffs of the W. S. Hoole Special Collections Library at the University of Alabama and at the Ben May Main Library in Mobile.

I am indebted to others for friendship, advice, and in some cases access to their historic houses. These include Rosemary B. Butler, Franklin Daugherty, Katherine Clark, W. Barksdale Maynard, Arthur Scully, Margaret Dixon, Sharon Williams, Dennis J. Knizley, Tyre Anderson, Carly Doughtery, Dr. Louie C. and Gail Wilson, Coll'ette King, Karen Beckwith, Dr. Donald L. and Ann Stone, Celia Lewis (for a lovely poem), Nicholas Holmes Jr., Nicholas Holmes III, David Newell, Roy Hoffman, E. C. LeVert, Tom Root, Palmer Hamilton, Rita K. Thompson, John Sims, Cammie East, Bailey du Mont, Jay Qualey, and Danielle Williams.

I want to particularly thank four individuals who read the book in manuscript and offered invaluable constructive criticism. Their services saved me from numerous embarrassments large and small. They are Douglas Kearley and Tom McGehee, who read with an eye to local historical matters, and Robert Mellown and Robert Gamble, who focused on broader architectural and historical themes.

The best photographer in Mobile, Sheila Hagler, and her friend and ally Peggy Denniston, have been, as ever, a pleasure and a joy to work with. Their talent, professionalism, and good humor have carried me over many a rough patch.

My admiration for Nicole Mitchell and her entire team at the University of Georgia Press is unbounded. Nicole has been our trusted editor and publisher for all three books, and her vision, sagacity, and European charm have made the experience one of the highlights of my professional career.

And then there is my family, without whom I would be truly lost. My wife, Lynn, to whom this book is dedicated, enriches my life every day, and her eagle editorial eye has made me a better writer. My children, Elena and Matthew, have always been tolerant of their father's love for history, and they have certainly done their time tramping through old buildings and cemeteries. Finally, I must thank my mother, Jeanne A. Sledge, whose love and support have never flagged through half a century. She brought me into this world, and with a devoted heart she has continued to cheer me on my way.

It should go without saying, but I'll say it nonetheless, any errors of fact herein are mine alone.

At the foot of Oakleigh's spiral staircase, 1993: Robert Denniston (center), one of the longest practicing attorneys in Mobile history, with his late brothers —Al (left), former president of Financiera Colón in Mexico, and George, former president of American National Bank in Mobile.

PHOTOGRAPHER'S NOTE

I became a photographer in a meager attempt to hold on to forever. Human memory is fragile, and often a photograph is what jogs the memory to recall cherished moments that would otherwise be lost. For example, my associate had forgotten about being a flower girl at age six until she saw the photograph I made at the front steps of Government Street Presbyterian Church from a child's viewpoint. The power of a photograph lies in its ability to connect the present with the past, joining people and events separated by time and space.

Which brings me to this: what is the significance of any given place, and why do we end up there? I have stalked the Oakleigh Mansion for more than a year now, thinking about the photograph to be made for this book. For me, the Oakleigh mansion is significant in two ways. First, I lived across the street for many years, and second, I work with the granddaughter of Harold Siebert Denniston, who remodeled Oakleigh and lived there with his family for nearly a quarter century.

Each time I visit, I recall the mid-1980s when I shared many hours with my two daughters on the lawn of Oakleigh — we lived across the street when they were just babies. Yesterday, my youngest (now twenty years old) asked: "Mom, why am I frightened to death of water? What happened to me to cause that?" (After all, mothers are supposed to know just about everything.) I explained that there is much about her early years I will never know. When she was four years old her family was fractured by divorce — she and her sister were forced to live in two households.

In 1924, a time long ago in a place far away, another family suffered a fractured life of a different kind. While living in La Paz, Bolivia, four-year-old Robert Denniston lost his mother, Lillian Pendaz Denniston. She died giving birth, and her newborn also died (this was the family's fourth loss). Deeply saddened, her husband, Harold Seibert Denniston, moved with his five children in early 1925 back to the United States, to Long Island, New York, and later that same year he married Florence Foster. Three years later, he moved his family to Mobile, Alabama, into their newly remodeled home, Oakleigh. Robert Denniston remembers almost nothing of his mother or his early years in Bolivia. But

If you pluck a special moment from life and frame it, are you defying death, decay and the passage of time or are you submitting to it?
—Orhan Pamuk, Istanbul: Memories and the City

during a recent visit he described vividly the day he, at the age of seven, and his family drove up to Oakleigh for the first time:

> We came up a long driveway to the back of a house I couldn't see for all the trees, where my father had created a new driveway from Roper Street. My father also added two new sets of stairs, a stairway in the back and one inside from the upper floor to the dining room on the first floor. Previously, the ground floor had been unoccupied, for the usual raised cottage type. He created the ground floor entirely. The front room was the "billiard room," with a full-sized pool table, and for his home office, and also had room for a regular poker table. Behind these were the dining room, and behind it a bedroom for George, another for Al and me, a kitchen, breakfast room, and storage closets. All of this was new.

On June 12, 2008, I positioned my tripod in the interior front room of Oakleigh. I didn't know it at the time, but my chosen vantage point was the exact place where Robert Denniston, as a child growing up at Oakleigh, shared many hours with his family gathered around a grand piano. His father, an accomplished musician and composer, played the piano "many evenings," Robert later told me. I bounced two incandescent lights off the ceiling and carefully proceeded to capture the photograph. A silent stillness filled the room but was suddenly broken when a docent began a tour. "This staircase was not original to the house," she said with a lovely southern drawl, from the entrance hallway at the top of the inside staircase. "It was put in by a family who bought the house in 1927. The man had the home remodeled to accommodate five young children." I was excited to hear the docent's talk, because although I was born and raised in Mobile, I had never heard the history of Oakleigh as told to visitors. "One of the children," she continued, "still lives in Mobile — an elderly gentleman now — and he wrote a five-page description of what it was like living here. They used to ride their bicycles downstairs. It was so big down there." She described the changes the family had made to the mansion, the family who had made this place home and preserved it for a quarter of a century.

For the past decade Peggy Denniston, one of four granddaughters of Harold Seibert "Denny" Denniston, and I have worked together as artists in residence in the Mobile County public schools, putting cameras in students' hands, compelling them to tell stories about their lives in words and pictures. She is a talented nonfiction writer, and through our partnership we have documented life in Lower Alabama through children's eyes. Our students' works have produced national touring exhibitions; a book, *The Eyes of the Storm*; and a documentary film project set in the post-Katrina Alabama coastal seafood villages of Bayou La Batre and Coden. Many years ago, when we first met, she told me, "My father grew up at Oakleigh." I didn't believe her at first. After all, Oakleigh is a museum. She told me the story of her amazing grandfather, and when she got out an original score of his, a waltz, and played it on the piano I was truly astonished. Denny was only a teenager when John Philip Sousa orchestrated that waltz and played it in Central Park with his band. Denny Denniston was a very talented man who not only was an expert musician but a champion sailor and brilliant businessman, who came to Mobile and started a third bank (disrupting the status quo of Old Mobile). His family gave Oakleigh life.

I cannot help but think, "What would have happened if Lillian hadn't died?" Denny's move into Oakleigh resulted from the death of his wife and child — very similar to the reason James Roper built the mansion: carrying on with life amid grief.

Sixty years after Robert Denniston's tiny hands slid down the rail of the spiral staircase, so did my children's hands, echoing the former presence of his and his siblings' — separated by so many years yet sharing the same structure, tiny hands on the curved rail.

Sheila Hagler

(Overleaf) View of the downtown from the Barton rotunda.

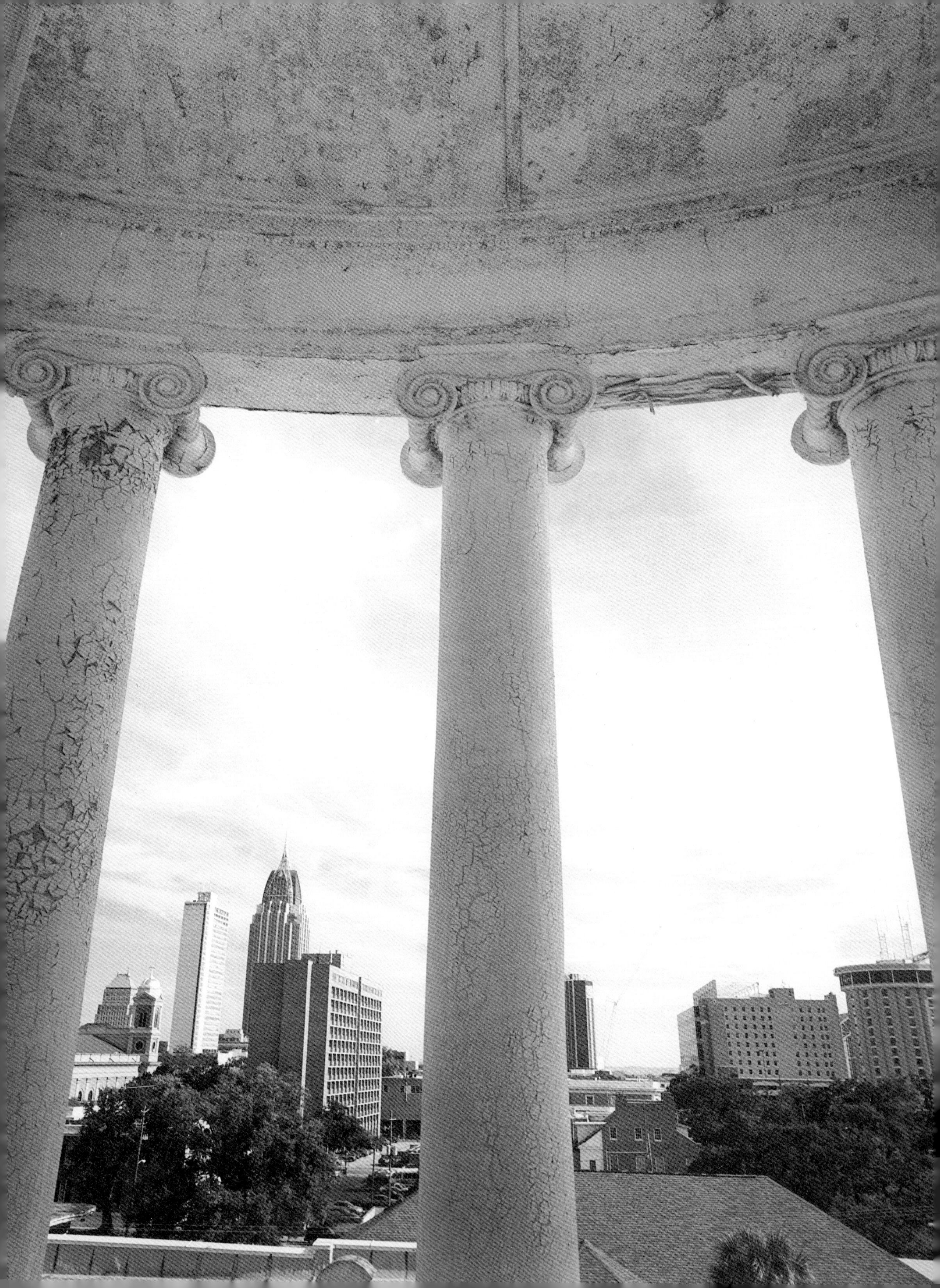

THE PILLARED CITY

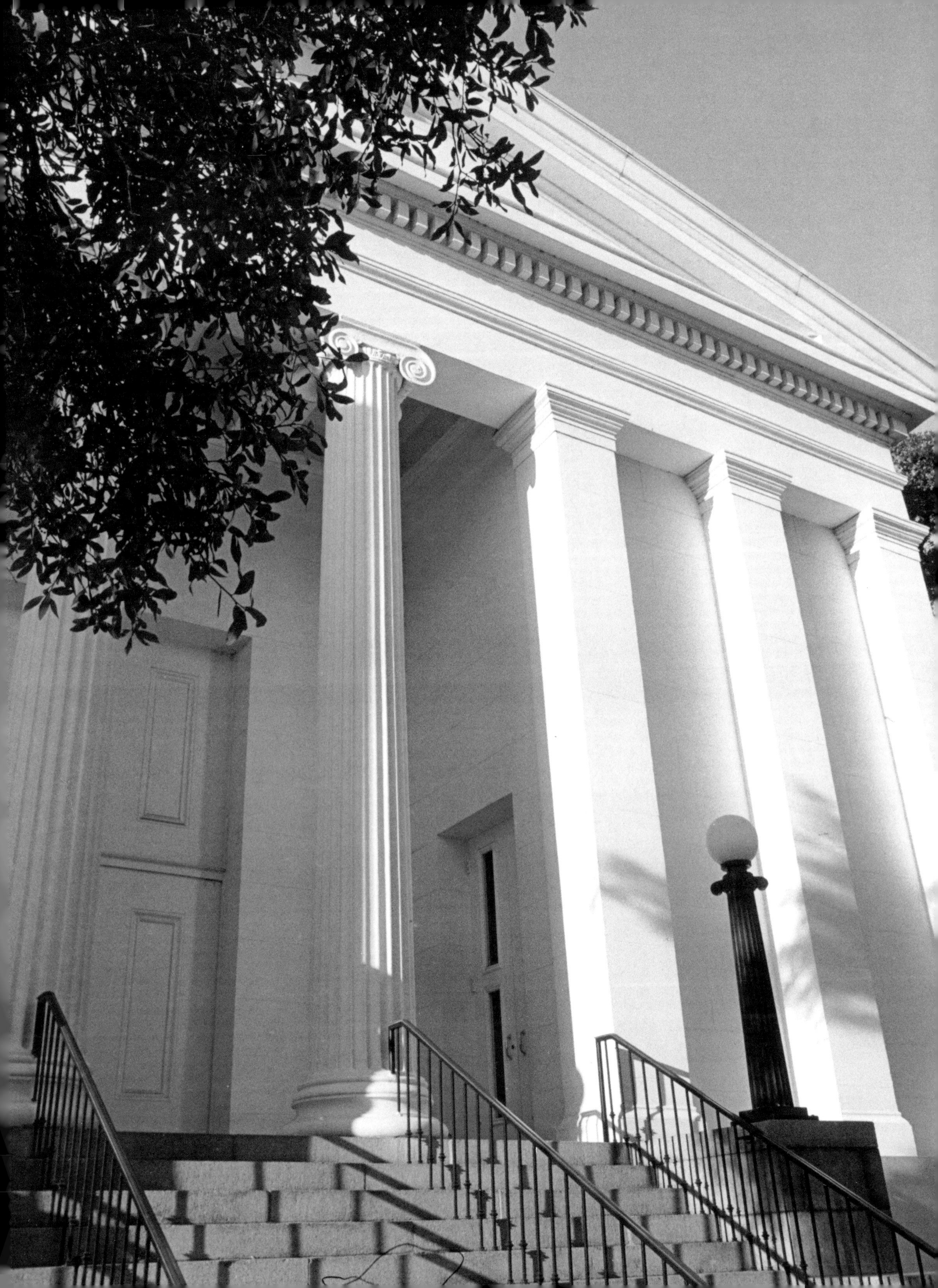

INTRODUCTION

GREEK REVIVAL ARCHITECTURE IN AMERICA

That the Hardaways chose to build Georgia Cottage in the Greek Revival style is hardly a surprise. From the 1820s to the Civil War, Americans exhibited an absolute mania for all things Grecian, especially in the decorative and building arts. Fired by the era's archaeological discoveries, Greece's independence fight against Turkey, prevailing European taste, and Americans' own hopeful new democracy, this was perhaps inevitable. Young boys learned their Greek in school, fashionable women sported high-waisted gowns, painters and sculptors employed classical motifs, and builders placed countless pillared edifices in many a newly founded Athens and Sparta.

In its purest form, Greek Revival architecture is defined by a masculinity and heaviness in massing and detail. Columns and pilasters are rendered in one of the three original orders — Doric, Ionic, or Corinthian — complete with full entablature and married to a low-pitched hip or pedimented roofline. The overall form is symmetrical, as in Georgia Cottage's central block and matching side wings. Interior elements are also robust and employ classical details like the acanthus leaf, palmette, dentil work, Greek key, and egg-and-dart molding. Architects and builders never intended to exactly copy the Greek temples and monuments that inspired the style but rather mixed and matched elements and details (including Roman innovations like the Tuscan and composite orders, the barrel vault, and the dome) as they saw fit and then fine-tuned them to geography and climate. The results were often breathtaking and became quintessentially American in their own right.

Seemingly every kind of building antebellum Americans needed lent itself to at least some classical interpretation or embellishment. From Maine to New Orleans, Massachusetts to Cincinnati, and South Carolina to Santa Fe, architects and builders erected Greek Revival state houses, courthouses, customs houses, jails, armories, engine houses, banks, offices, schools, hospitals, hotels, churches, town houses, plantation mansions, cottages, barns, privies, and even some slave houses. Little wonder that when Samuel F. Smith wrote the lyrics to the hymn

(Opposite) Government Street Presbyterian Church lends a strong classical dignity to busy Government Street.

(Left) The Doric Order. From Asher Benjamin, The Architect, or Practical House Carpenter, *1830.*

(Center) The Ionic Order. From Asher Benjamin, The Architect, or Practical House Carpenter, *1830.*

(Right) The Corinthian Order. From Asher Benjamin, The Architect, or Practical House Carpenter, *1830.*

America in 1832, he rhapsodized over the "woods and templed hills" that so distinguished the young republic.[1]

Mobilians like the Hardaways — that is, people of taste, means, and culture — embraced the Greek Revival as enthusiastically as their countrymen did, and beginning in the 1830s, their city blossomed with columns, pediments, architraves, and rotundas. As early as 1839, the town's sandy streets boasted more than a dozen significant examples of the style, including three churches, a school, two hotels, a bank, a hospital, and several residences. Even though other antebellum styles, like the Italianate and Gothic Revival, eventually took root in Mobile, none so thoroughly symbolized civic pride and ambition as did the Greek Revival. Besides its formal expression in high-style public buildings, Greek Revival was also readily and successfully blended with indigenous building traditions to create unique and pleasing variations.

Some very capable researchers have already studied and written about historic Mobile architecture, most notably Elizabeth Barrett Gould in two books, *From Fort to Port: An Architectural History of Mobile, Alabama, 1711–1918* (1988) and *From Builders to Architects: The Hobart-Hutchisson Six* (1997), and Robert Gamble in his compilation *The Alabama Catalog: A Guide to the Early Architecture of the State* (1987). Adhering to rigorous professional standards, these scholars concentrated on the physical characteristics of numerous architectural styles across a broad time span but underplayed the important human elements of the story. What this book attempts to do is present the saga of one particularly rich period in the history of Mobile's built environment, the Greek Revival (ca. 1825–70), more comprehensively and colorfully than ever before, with cognizance of the modest as well as the grand, and hopefully instilling in the reader a better appreciation for this distinctive style and a commitment to historic preservation as a civic priority. How financial boom and bust, destructive fires, pestilence, war, and almost superhuman determination, skill, and talent across two centuries impacted Greek Revival Mobile is a fascinating and intriguing story that has never been fully told. As with any local historical subject, this one is inseparable from the broader national epic of which it is a small but fascinating part.

NEOCLASSICAL ANTECEDENTS

The Greek Revival style did not appear full-blown on the American scene but rather evolved out of a centuries-old neoclassical tradition. Since the Renaissance at least, European building taste had been profoundly influenced by ancient Roman architecture, which was considered the highest manifestation of the art. Greek architecture, by contrast, was perceived as a pale precursor. Architects like Andrea Palladio (1508–80) of Italy and after him Inigo Jones (1573–1652) and Christopher Wren (1632–1723) of England and the Scottish brothers Robert (1728–92) and James Adam (1732–94) studied the Roman landmarks and successfully employed columns, arches, domes, rotundas, dentils, quoins, and balustrades on churches, hospitals, palaces, town houses, and country homes.[2]

By the mid-eighteenth century, a significant shift in attitude occurred, when architects and philosophers began to conceive of ancient Greece as more than a mere stepping stone to Roman civilization, but as a rich culture unto itself, whose fine building heritage was worthy of study and emulation. This shift was occasioned by several factors, including archaeological discoveries and learned publications that spread this knowledge. As scholars delved into their work, a greater admiration and respect for Greece emerged, and it came to be regarded as the fountainhead. Wrote one author, "Architecture has only middling obligations to the Romans, and . . . owes all that is precious and solid to the Greeks alone."[3]

CATALYST

The Greek Revival style's most important catalyst was a four-book set, *The Antiquities of Athens*, published between 1762 and 1816. The authors were a pair of British antiquarians, James Stuart and Nicholas Revett, who had visited Greece in the early 1750s to measure and draw its ancient landmarks. Their trip was sponsored by the Society of Dilettanti, an organization theretofore better

*The Kennedy House has long graced downtown Mobile
with its stately white pillars and arched windows.*

known for its debaucheries than its cultural achievements. The English politician and author Horace Walpole joked that in order to be a member, "the nominal qualification is having been in Italy, and the real one, having been drunk."[4]

Nonetheless, Stuart and Revett were earnest about their project and, with sketchbooks and measuring tapes, clambered over the Parthenon, the Erechtheum, the Temple of Theseus, the Tower of the Winds, and other famous Grecian ruins. Their drawings were notable not only for their inherent romantic charm but for painstaking accuracy and precision. These were representations easily copied in stone or wood by contemporary builders and carpenters, a fact very much to the fore in Stuart and Revett's thinking. In the preface to the first volume, they wrote that anyone with an interest in the arts "must be infinitely more pleased, and better instructed, the nearer they can draw their Examples, from the Fountain-head."[5]

The work made its authors famous — Stuart became known ever after as "Athenian" Stuart — and its impact on Western European architecture was immediate and electric. As one early nineteenth-century British architect recalled, "No event that ever occurred in the history of architecture . . . produced so sudden, decided, and beneficial effect as did the works of James Stuart."[6] From Russia to Germany to Britain, Grecian-inspired pillared and pedimented landmarks arose, including the Admiralty at St. Petersburg (1806–23), the Brandenburg Gate (1788–91), and the British Museum (1823–48).[7]

AMERICAN GENESIS

Like all other formal nineteenth-century building fashions, the Greek Revival came late to America's shores. Influenced by British examples, beautiful neoclassical buildings had been erected during the late eighteenth century, particularly by men like Charles Bullfinch (1763–1844), whose public buildings and residential commissions displayed a pleasing lightness and grace. Omnivore that he was, Thomas Jefferson owned a copy of Stuart and Revett but as a builder preferred to work exclusively in the Roman métier, as demonstrated by Monticello (1793–1809), the Virginia state house (1798), and the University of Virginia (1817–26). These buildings represent the epitome of early American classicism — trim and delicate in feel, with lovely fanlights and soothing proportions.[8]

It would fall to the British-born architect Benjamin Henry Latrobe to design America's first arguably Greek Revival building, the Bank of Pennsylvania (1799–1801) in Philadelphia. In a letter to Jefferson penned on May 21, 1807, Latrobe famously declared: "My principles of good taste are rigid in Grecian architecture. I am a bigoted Greek in the condemnation of Roman architecture. . . . Whenever, therefore, the Grecian style can be copied without impropriety,

I love to be a mere, I would say a slavish copyist."[9] Despite this contention, Latrobe's Bank of Pennsylvania was anything but pure Greek — he employed fanlight transoms and a low dome — but his graceful Ionic porticos and strong pedimented rooflines at front and rear were what dominated the view from below and most impressed passersby.

It was, in fact, a native Philadelphian who became the Greek Revival's greatest American champion. Nicholas Biddle, a financier and man of well-cultivated taste, visited Greece in 1806, one of the first Americans to do so. His interest in the ancient world dated from childhood, as he confessed in his journal: "I had long felt an ardent desire to visit Greece. The fate of a nation whose history was the first brilliant object that met my infancy, and the first foundation of my early studies was so interesting that I had resolved to avail myself of any opportunity of witnessing it. The soil of Greece is sacred to Genius and to letters."[10]

While there, Biddle, like Stuart and Revett before him, seriously applied himself to the study and measurement of architecture. In his journal he described the Parthenon, or Temple of Minerva, as he called it, as "fine ruins — 100 feet broad, 227 long, 69 high. The order Doric, the marble Pentelique, and its original whiteness has been softened by the yellow tinge perhaps peculiar to this country." The building's sad state he considered a monument "of our littleness and our grandeur."[11] Upon his return to America Biddle asserted, "There are but two truths in this world, the Bible and Greek architecture," and he diligently set about doing everything he could to promote the latter in his native city.[12]

THE LIONS OF PHILADELPHIA

Philadelphia proved to be fertile soil for the Greek Revival. In addition to Biddle's advocacy (especially after his 1819 appointment as president of the United States Bank, when his influence and power were considerable), there was the favorable public opinion of Latrobe's Bank of Pennsylvania; the presence of the Franklin Institute, whose journal featured articles on classical taste; and a talented coterie of young architects who smelled money and were eager to demonstrate their mastery of the craft.[13]

Between 1812 and 1836, so many prominent Greek Revival buildings were erected in Philadelphia that they became known collectively as "the lions" and were a popular tourist attraction. Among the first and most impressive of these landmarks was the Fairmount Waterworks, constructed on the banks of the Schuylkill River between 1812 and 1822. Designed by Frederick Graff, an engineer who had worked at Latrobe's elbow, the waterworks included an engine house, mill house, and promenade above the dam. Distinguished by porticoes, colonnades, and state-of-the-art technology in the massive waterwheels, the

The old City Hospital was among the first Greek Revival structures to be erected in Mobile.

Fairmount Waterworks instantly marked Philadelphia as a town where innovation and exciting design could find a welcome home.[14]

Almost as important as the Waterworks, perhaps more so from a design standpoint, was the Second Bank of the United States, authored by the American-born architect William Strickland and erected between 1819 and 1824. Strickland had been a student of Latrobe and was a particular favorite of Biddle, who almost certainly played a deciding role in awarding him the commission. When the bank's directors announced the design competition for their new headquarters to be built on Chestnut Street, they requested "a chase [sic] imitation of Grecian Architecture, in its simplest and least expensive form."[15]

Strickland gave them exactly what they wanted, a virtual copy of the Parthenon lifted straight from the pages of Stuart and Revett. Its construction required sophisticated and skilled coordination, as well as jaw-dropping quantities of building supplies and material — 41,500 cubic feet of stone, 17.5 tons of copper for the roof, 250 bushels of plastering hair, 175 loads of gravel, 2 gilt platinum lightning rods, and almost 800 feet of mahogany for the furniture. The finished product commanded attention with its eight massive Doric columns and strong pediment, and it became a design template for branch banks elsewhere in the country.[16]

Other important Greek Revival buildings tumbled forth from the drafting tables. These included the Merchants' Exchange (1831–33), also by Strickland, which sported a curved colonnade and a replica of the Choragic Monument of Lysicrates atop; and Girard College (1833–47), where Biddle was a trustee, designed by Thomas U. Walter (who had studied with Strickland), with a peripteral Corinthian colonnade sheltering 38,000 square feet of interior space. Walter also worked with Biddle on upgrading the latter's personal residence on the Delaware River, Andalusia, with a hexastyle Doric portico and full-blown entablature.[17]

These buildings' rapid and stunning appearance, as well as Biddle's national prominence during the 1830s "bank war" with President Andrew Jackson, assured a great deal of public interest. Both the famous and the hoi polloi made the rounds, and many wrote down their impressions. Fanny Trollope, mother of the famous British novelist Anthony Trollope, commented on both Latrobe's and Strickland's banks as well as on the Fairmount Waterworks. The banks she considered "the most striking buildings," while the Waterworks presented "a lovely scene."[18] The Waterworks likewise awed Charles Dickens. "Philadelphia is most bountifully provided with fresh water," he explained in his generally grumpy account of his American tour, "which is showered and jerked about, and turned on, and poured off, everywhere. The Waterworks, which are on a height near the city, are no less ornamental than useful, being tastefully laid out as a public garden, and kept in the best and neatest order."[19]

J. S. Buckingham, a British aristocrat who saw the city in 1840, enthused over all the lions. The Second Bank he pronounced "one of the best specimens of the Doric, in the purest times of Greek architecture, to be seen anywhere out of Greece itself." Contemplating Girard College he wrote, "In no country have I ever seen, either among the ruins of ancient or the works of modern days, a more beautiful structure than this, or one in which chasteness of design, richness of decoration, and exquisite skill of workmanship were more happily combined; yet every part of it is of unassisted American execution." Finally, at the Waterworks he praised the combination of "beauty, simplicity, and utility."[20]

Throughout the 1830s and 1840s the travelers kept coming and kept sharing their reactions. In the October 1836 edition of *The North American Review*, an anonymous writer praised the banks and the Merchants' Exchange, and then waxed eloquent on the virtues of the Doric order in particular, which seemed "to bid defiance to the elements and to time itself."[21]

Philip Hone, a merchant and former mayor of New York City, traveled through Philadelphia in February 1838 and was beguiled after a nocturnal ramble around the Second Bank. Hone described its gently illuminated facade in his diary: "each of the massive fluted columns had a jet of light from the inner side so placed as not to be seen from the street, but casting a strong light upon the front of the building, the softness of which, with its flickering from the wind, produced an effect strikingly beautiful."[22] Clergymen proved just as susceptible to the city's Grecian allure. Henry Whipple, an Episcopal bishop from Minnesota heading to warmer climes, toured the lions in 1844 and especially admired Girard College, which he considered "one of the finest structures in the Union."[23]

Even as late as 1855, when the Greek Revival was long past apogee and other architectural styles dotted the Philadelphia landscape, travelers still exulted over the city's classical appearance. John W. Oldmixon, an English visitor, was delighted by the "great profusion of white marble everywhere — door-steps, sills of windows and frames, door-jambs, pilasters, columns, cornices, pediments on all the facades in profusion, and everywhere perfectly bright and clean."[24]

BUILDING IN ANTEBELLUM AMERICA

Despite what the lions seemed to indicate, the study and practice of American architecture during the mid-nineteenth century was largely an immature craft. The most common method of study was to attach oneself to an established architect and learn on the job. Fortunately for those who aspired to build, there were many immigrant British architects capable of imparting a great deal of

The Lowery-Garner House (1851) at 1156 Church Street is one of the city's most refined Gulf Coast cottages. Its eared door and window architraves, boxed columns, and dentil work are nicely applied to the much older cottage form, creating a near perfect balance of the high style and vernacular.

both formal and useful knowledge. Men like Latrobe, William Jay, Richard Upjohn, and James Gallier Sr. were eager to pass on what they knew and further the young profession in their adopted homeland.

In his autobiography, Gallier provided insight into his European architectural education, obtained at the School of Fine Arts in Dublin and on his own. The school was only open three days a week for two hours each day, he recalled, and wanting to learn more, he took matters into his own hands. "I now filled up every spare hour I could get at copying the orders of architecture and such other details as I could find at the academy; and, although there was but very little instruction given at the school, I there got the first glimpse of the way in which drawings were made."[25] Gallier also roamed around England, doing joinery and carpentry work, learning the practical skills that would advance his career.

But when he immigrated to New York in 1832, just as the Greek Revival was beginning to flower, he found his prospects complicated by the fact that "the majority of the people could with difficulty be made to understand what was meant by a professional architect; the builders, that is, the carpenters and bricklayers, all called themselves architects."[26] To his further distress, Gallier found that many people preferred to hire "some poor draftsman" for a pittance and then put up the building themselves or, worse, not resort to any plans at all but simply find a building they liked and attempt to copy it.[27]

Nothing spread architectural knowledge or the Greek Revival faster than the proliferation of pattern books during the early nineteenth century. Among the most important and influential were Asher Benjamin's *The Architect, or Practical House Carpenter* (1830) and Minard Lafever's *The Beauties of Modern Architecture* (1835). Benjamin's treatise included detailed drawings of the classical orders and such minutiae as "The method of drawing Greek and Roman moldings," "The method of fluting and diminishing columns," and "The method of gluing up and finishing shafts of columns."[28] Himself an architect, Benjamin was also an evangelist for disseminating correct knowledge. "I consider it necessary that all practical house carpenters should be fully acquainted with the orders of architecture," he wrote in his introduction. Benjamin was confident that his precise drawings would make even "a workman of ordinary capacity" a "perfect master of the orders."[29]

Lafever, a talented draftsman and architect who had partnered briefly with Gallier, also included illustrations of the orders, as well as mantel, door, and window details and ceiling molds. Like Benjamin, he hoped that his book would enable the "operative workman" to "become a complete master of his business."[30] Lafever's drawings also exhibited a subtle originality. In describing his plate of an Ionic capital, he wrote, "This capital is not of any particular specimen of antique productions, but partakes of several, as well as of fancy." Overall, he thought it presented "rather a pleasing effect."[31] With pattern books like Benjamin's and Lafever's in hand, nineteenth-century builders were capable of astonishing quality in town or country.

The construction of even a modest Greek Revival building was an involved enterprise. Besides an architect, master builder, or some kind of supervisor, numerous tradesmen (often called mechanics) were needed to do the job. These included masons, carpenters, joiners (who assembled the finer woodwork like windows, doors, mantels, wainscoting, and furniture), plasterers, painters, roofers, and laborers. A surprisingly diverse and sophisticated range of building materials and tools was available to nineteenth-century workmen — many varieties of wood like cypress, poplar, cedar, pine, and oak, which America had in great abundance; good quality stone and clays for brick; lead-based paint; wrought and cast iron for limited structural or ornamental use; cheap nails; and many kinds of hammers, mallets, augers, drills, chisels, saws, planers, and paintbrushes.

(Opposite) The Tardy Cottage (1858) at 104 South Lawrence Street demonstrates the enduring popularity of the older Gulf Coast cottage form even as the Italianate and Greek Revival began to merge midcentury.

One carpenter's guide from the era lists a dizzying array of saws available — the ripping saw (to cut with the grain); a panel saw (for cabinetry work); tenon, sash, and dovetail saws (smaller pistol-gripped woodworking instruments); and the compass saw and keyhole, or turning, saw (for tight work).[32]

Despite these advantages, the hours for workmen were long, the tasks sometimes dangerous, and extremes of heat and cold took their toll. In his autobiography, Gallier recalled his work on the St. Charles Hotel in New Orleans and the reforms he instituted for the workingmen, who on that project numbered in the hundreds. Gallier introduced "the system of ten hours' labour for a day's work; this was hailed by the men as a great amelioration, as the custom up to that time had been to work from sunrise to sunset." He also started paying the hands their full wages every two weeks, which made him so popular, he claimed, that he had his pick of top men. Gallier subcontracted specialty work like the masonry, plastering, slating, and ironwork "to persons already established in those several trades."[33]

The basic steps in erecting a frame Greek Revival house were remarkably similar, whether the locale was Maine, Minnesota, Ohio, or Georgia. There were, of course, numerous regional nuances dictated by climate and custom — Georgia's Greek Revival houses more often display hip roofs, Ohio's front-facing gables — but the essential work plan was the same. First, footings were dug into the soil (in the coastal South cypress boards were sometimes employed as a floating foundation); brick piers were then constructed, held together with a lime and sand mortar mix. Next, carpenters laid down the massive sills and floor joists and pegged the larger pieces together with wooden tree nails. In order to do this, the carpenter expertly fashioned a mortise and tenon joint using an array of tools specially designed for the purpose. The walls and roof were framed up, chimneys constructed, and the portico, if there was one, decked and ceiled. The front columns could either be boxed or round, and were usually fashioned of wood, though some were brick with stucco fluting. The capitals were wood or, more rarely on residences, stone, pot metal, or cast iron. The siding, or weatherboarding, was hammered onto the framing with square nails. Then came the roofing, usually wooden shingles affixed onto wide, wooden-slat decking with smaller nails. Floors were tongue-and-groove and were sometimes very roughly laid. *The Economic Cottage Builder* of 1856 explained that this was the usual practice, "as it is customary to carpet every room in the house."[34]

Next came the mantels, baseboards, cabinetry, doors, and windows with their casings and shutters. These were usually stock elements, ordered from sash and door outfits that more and more towns had as the nineteenth century advanced. Strips of wooden lath applied to the framing served as a base for the plaster, though some houses had simple wood plank walls. Painters then went to work

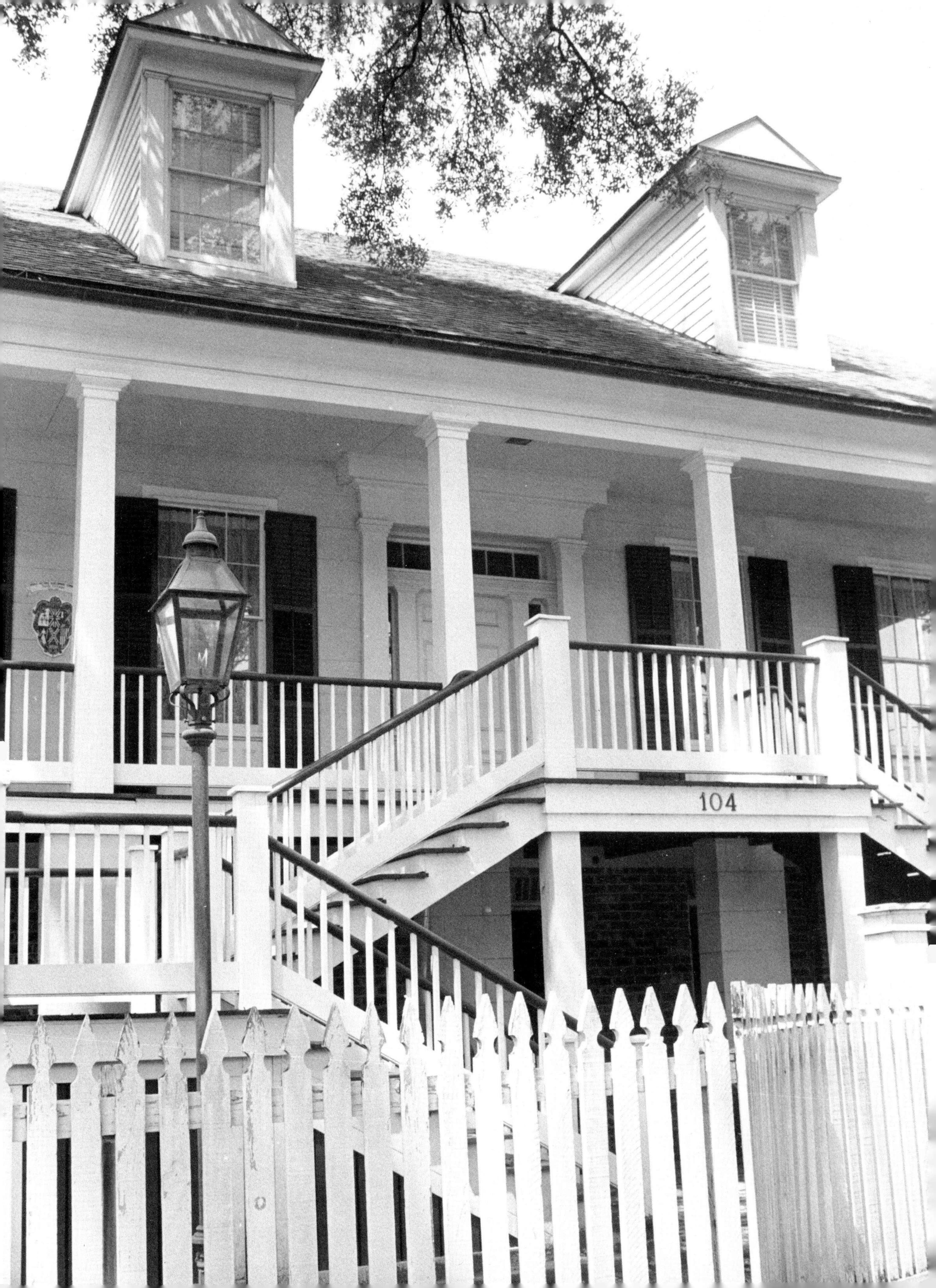
104

inside and out. Interior walls and trim were usually white or off-white, though occasionally other colors were used. The exterior also displayed a limited palette. The body of most frame Greek Revival houses was usually white (or sometimes gray or blue), with black-green shutters (sometimes the top rail on the porch balustrade was also done to match), and light-blue porch ceilings. Lastly, interior decorative finishes like graining or marbling (techniques to make a surface, usually wood, stucco, or plaster, appear to be finer wood or marble), and hardware (locks, doorknobs, shutter dogs) were added.

There was, of course, no electricity in those days, and indoor plumbing was almost unheard of but for the wealthiest. Lighting was by gas, whale oil, candle, sun, or moon, and chamber pots or outhouses were the rule for rich and poor alike. Because of the omnipresent danger of fire, kitchens were detached.

All done and dried out, the house was ready to be furnished. Throughout the antebellum period, Empire furniture was the dominant style, and its large, masculine scale blended easily into the Greek Revival's spacious interiors. In her book, Fanny Trollope went into great detail about the interior of a New York house she visited. "Silk or satin furniture is as often, or oftener, seen than chintz," she wrote. The mirrors she thought as fine as any she'd seen in London, and she concluded by describing the "little tables, looking and smelling like flower beds, portfolios, nick-nacks, bronzes, busts, cameos, and alabaster vases, illustrated copies of ladylike rhymes bound in silk, and, in short, all the pretty coxcomalities of the drawing-room scattered about with the same profuse and studied negligence as with us."[35]

Landscaping provided the final touch, and particularly in the rural South, this had a great deal to do with how houses were perceived. In general, like the buildings themselves, strong, symmetrical, and linear were the guiding principles. Evergreens like cypress, cedar, and yew were favorites, and camellias, tea olive, banana shrub, crape myrtle, and wisteria dotted the grounds. Town houses sometimes featured flower boxes, though Mrs. Trollope thought the practice not as prevalent as in London and Paris.[36]

Taken in toto, the Greek Revival house was a markedly superior dwelling. Modern restorers often profess admiration for the quality of workmanship exhibited in these old buildings. Yet even as far back as 1871, knowledgeable observers were aware that a gulf yawned between the antebellum and postwar years. A writer for the *Manufacturer and Builder* commented on the older windows and doors he had examined. "What was the secret of their good workmanship?" he asked. "It lay in the fact that the timber that composed them was well selected and well seasoned, and not what was lifted from the timber-pond the day previously. Their making was also not a job against time, a sort of hurry-skurry, slap-dash, break-neck 'slap-work.'"[37]

NEW YORK AND BEYOND

Given the young nation's explosive internal growth, the abundance of quality building materials at the ready, and the profusion of talented builders armed with architectural pattern books, the Greek Revival style flourished everywhere. Besides Philadelphia, one of the other early centers was New York City, where a clutch of capable and aggressive architects was based. No firm played so influential a role in the style's development, not only in New York but even as far away as the Gulf Coast, as that of Town and Davis. Established in 1829 by Ithiel Town, a forty-four-year-old architect and engineer famous for the invention of the Town truss, and Alexander Jackson Davis, a twenty-six-year-old artist and draftsman who would eventually be a leading light in American architecture, this firm became a seedbed of innovation, taste, and style.[38]

The very year the firm was founded, it took in a young member who would soon carry what he had learned to the distant cities of Mobile and New Orleans. James Dakin, a native New Yorker, was only twenty-three years old, recently married, and eager to put his love of architecture to practical use. While working with Town and Davis, he absorbed a number of clever improvements on the Greek Revival style, including something called "pilastrades." These replaced the expensive peripteral columns of classical Greece with a series of massive pilasters along the sides of a building, thus providing an acceptable semblance of rhythm and form at a significant savings of space and money. From this came a special kind of window — which Davis, alert to his own importance in these matters, labeled "Davisean" — designed to fill the space between the pilastrades and provide the necessary light and air to the interior. Town and Davis also exploited the immensely practical distyle in antis configuration for church facades. Consisting of a pair of large columns set between pilasters or thick walls, this arrangement gave a building the appearance of monumentality while avoiding the wasted space of an attached, full portico. The interior spaces within the flanking walls were thus available for vestibules or staircases leading to basement and balcony. Town and Davis's Carmine Street Presbyterian Church (1831) demonstrated both the usefulness and popularity of these design improvements. The resulting building, though hardly pure Greek, certainly looked good and amply proved that classical elements could be adaptively employed by inventive brains.[39]

Besides James Dakin, other young builders worked for Town and Davis. In May 1832, James Gallier briefly joined the firm. In his autobiography he remembered the strengths and weaknesses of his new employers. "Town had been a carpenter, but was no draftsman," he wrote. "Davis, his partner, was no mechanic, but was a good draftsman, and possessed much taste as an artist; he had furnished the plans for many of the public buildings in some of the States at that time." Gallier was particularly impressed by Dakin, whom he considered "a young man of genius." In addition to these men's considerable practical experience, Gallier noted that the office also contained "a very respectable library," which Town had acquired during several trips to London.[40]

In 1833 Gallier left the firm to work with Lafever, and Dakin brought in his younger brother Charles as a draftsman. Things didn't remain settled for long, however. In October 1834 Charles Dakin and Gallier went South in search of greater opportunities, and a little over a year later, James Dakin joined them.[41]

Architects and builders like these men, foreign and native born, of varying degrees of skill and training, penetrated every corner of the land. North, south, east, and west, Greek Revival buildings peppered the American landscape. Notable landmarks, many of which still stand, include the Baltimore Cathedral (1804–18) by Latrobe; Arlington House in Virginia, built in 1804, with a massive Doric portico added in 1818, by George Hadfield; Savannah's Scarbrough House (1819) by William Jay; the Washington, D.C., Patent Office (1836–40) and Treasury Department (1836–42) by Robert Mills; the Alsop House (1838) in Connecticut by Ithiel Town, which features a T-shaped plan for better ventilation; the Lyceum (1848) on the University of Mississippi campus in Oxford by William Nichols; Waverly (1852) in Columbus, Mississippi, architect unknown; and state houses in Alabama, Arkansas, Connecticut, Florida, Georgia, Illinois, Kentucky, Maine, Mississippi, North Carolina, Ohio, Tennessee, and Vermont.

Some American towns presented a decidedly classical appearance, and people noticed. A British traveler on the Mississippi River in 1835 was pleased by his first glimpse of Baton Rouge, Louisiana. "The view from the deck of the steamer is highly beautiful," he wrote. "The rich, green swells rising gradually from the water — its pleasant streets, bordered with the umbrageous China tree — its colonnaded dwellings — its mingled town and rural scenary [sic], and its pleasant suburbs, give it an air of quiet and novel beauty."[42] In an 1861 article for *DeBow's Review*, an anonymous writer commented on Natchez, Mississippi's "classic antiquity."[43]

Alabama, enjoying the riches of the cotton boom, provided an extraordinary stage for the Greek Revival, and not surprisingly it proliferated there. A handful of fine buildings around the state already exhibited a high degree of classicism — the old capitol in Tuscaloosa (1828–30) by William Nichols; the Forks of Cypress in Florence (ca. 1830), also by Nichols and featuring a gorgeous fanlight and peripteral colonnade; and Mobile's Spring Hill College (1831) by Claude Beroujon.[44] The public was also primed, having heard and read Greek architecture extolled by orators and newspapers. In April 1831, the *Alabama Intelligencer and States Rights Expositor* of Tuscaloosa praised the Parthenon, "The holiest and most magnificent ruin the world contains," to its readers. The article went on to describe "the flutings of the columns, the swelling of the capitals, and all the endless ornaments of the architrave, frieze and cornice!" It may be debated how familiar the readership was with these architectural terms, but the paper felt no need to define them.[45]

Builders' familiarity with a classical vocabulary is evident from old construction records. In the contract for Magnolia Hall, an 1850 mansion erected in Greensboro by Benjamin F. Parsons, a Massachusetts-born architect, the details are quite specific. "The Porticoes are to be in the Grecian Ionic Order," the document reads, "and the Entablature and Mouldings all to harmonize with it."[46] Parsons, of course, knew these terms, but it is not brash to presume that David F. McCrary, the builder, and the ordinary workmen knew them, too, and understood how everything was supposed to fit together.

Grand, columned buildings arose from Huntsville to Mobile. The new state capitol, erected in Montgomery in 1850 (Daniel Pratt, architect) remains a landmark example of the style, as do Gaineswood (1842–60, Nathan Bryan Whitfield, owner/architect) in Demopolis and Sturdivant Hall (1854, Thomas Helm Lee, master builder) in Selma.[47]

Not everyone could afford to work or live in such splendor, however. For thousands of poor whites, yeoman farmers, and planters just starting out, rougher lodgings were the norm — single or double pen log cabins; saddleback, dogtrot, or I-houses — though sometimes a little Greek Revival touch could be found around a doorway or gracing a porch. For slaves throughout the South, housing was even more rudimentary, with precious little decoration or style at all. A traveler through Alabama in 1860 penned a woeful description that may serve for untold other locales. "Their huts, to me," he wrote, "look wretched in the extreme, with not a pane of glass, not a particle of green turf, not a flower or a shrub, not an outbuilding of any kind, not the slightest indication of anything which we, at the North, call comfort."[48]

CONTEMPORARY REACTIONS

As with any pervasive cultural phenomenon, America's passion for Greek Revival architecture provoked a great deal of commentary. Members of the building community and the general public weighed in, debating the merits of copying ancient Greek architecture. For his part, Latrobe bristled at the accusation that his Bank of Pennsylvania was an unimaginative knockoff. Perhaps forgetting his "slavish copyist" remark to Jefferson of some years earlier, he wrote, "All that is said on this subject is as absurd as it is false, even the Porticos vary

Attic detail, Government Street Presbyterian Church. This image clearly reveals the meticulous construction methodology behind the interior's coffered ceiling.

in every part of their proportions of columns and entablature from every temple in existence."[49] In 1841 Thomas U. Walter defended his work in the style. "The popular idea that to design a building in Grecian taste is nothing more than to copy a Grecian building is altogether erroneous," he wrote. "Even the Greeks themselves never made two buildings alike." He then went to the heart of what he believed made a good architect: "If architects would oftener *think* as the Greeks thought, than to *do* as the Greeks did, our columnar architecture would possess a higher degree of originality and its character and expression would gradually conform to the local circumstances of the country and the republican spirit of its institutions."[50]

Despite such eloquent justifications, the detractors had a field day. In his 1838 novel *Home as Found*, James Fenimore Cooper was wickedly dismissive. "One such temple well placed in a wood, might be a pleasant object enough," one of his characters says, "but to see a river lined with them, with children trundling hoops before their doors, beef carried into their kitchens, and smoke issuing, moreover, from those unclassical objects, chimnies, is too much even of a high taste; one might as well live in a fever."[51]

In the summer of 1850, an anonymous writer for the *New Englander and Yale Review* was equally disparaging. He mocked those rich enough to hire a carpenter "who has heard of the five orders and owns a 'Builder's Guide,' and forthwith will be seen to go up a Grecian temple in clapboards with its kitchen and cooking apparatus at one end and its prim fluted columns at the other! A temple of Minerva with its sauce-pans and pianos!"[52]

The tide had irrevocably turned by the fall of 1859, when *Harper's New Monthly Magazine* announced, "The Greek mania has pretty much run out, and the Gothic mania has taken its place."[53] Though Americans would continue to erect Greek Revival buildings up to and even beyond the Civil War, other architectural styles were ascendant, including the medieval-inspired Gothic Revival and the Italianate with its elaborate evocations of Renaissance Italy.

As the nineteenth century advanced, and high Victorian styles like the Second Empire, Romanesque Revival, and Queen Anne introduced an astonishing busyness to the built environment, kinder attitudes toward the Greek Revival emerged. Mrs. Schuyler Van Rensselaer, a cultural pundit writing for the *Century* in May 1884, struck a tolerant tone. She wrote that the older Greek Revival courthouse or church evident in so many American towns "is usually a far better thing in itself, and far more agreeable in its testimony to the taste if not to the practical wisdom of its builders, than is its later neighbor — a bastard structure with vulgarized reminiscences of many styles and no styles, and much riotous ornamentation in sanded zinc and jig-saw carving."[54] At century's end there was even a resurgence of neoclassicism in American architecture, but significant differences are evident between these buildings and their antebellum cousins. In general, the Neoclassical Revival buildings exhibit an increased dependence on the Corinthian and Roman orders and overall are more florid and less well proportioned. The Greek Revival's day had indeed passed, but nostalgia was not long in coming.

WHITE PILLARS IN THE MOONLIGHT

As early as the 1880s, the Greek Revival style began to be romanticized, especially by southern writers. In the popular imagination, it soon became a southern phenomenon, and the image of white pillars in the moonlight instantly evoked a culture swept away.

The folklorist and journalist Joel Chandler Harris was among the first to establish this linkage. In his book *Nights with Uncle Remus: Myths and Legends of the Old Plantation* (1883) he wrote of a "stately house on a wooded hill, the huge white pillars . . . rising high enough to catch the reflection of a rosy sunset."[55] Other romancers included Thomas Nelson Page, who wrote of a time when

A fallen column at the Hall-Ford House reveals its brick and stucco construction.

"even the moonlight was richer and mellower." In his popular book *In Ole Virginia* (1881) he movingly described decaying, columned mansions overlooking empty, fallow lands.[56]

In the first half of the twentieth century, southern writers employed the Greek Revival as a compelling symbol of broken power and decadence. William Faulkner's *Sartoris* (1929) brilliantly conjured the interior of the aristocrat John Sartoris's home. "The stairway with its white spindles and red carpet mounted in a tall slender curve into upper gloom," Faulkner wrote. He went on to describe the main parlor "emanating an atmosphere of dim and seldom violated stateliness." Its tall mirror, Faulkner concluded, was "filled with grave obscurity like a still pool of evening water."[57] Stark Young's 1934 novel *So Red the Rose* was equally evocative and sold in greater numbers than Faulkner's more difficult work.

But nothing so cemented the connection between Greek Revival architecture and the slave South as did the movie version of Margaret Mitchell's *Gone with the Wind*, which premiered in 1939. Millions of Americans were enthralled by the big-screen spectacle of belles, beaux, and humble slaves against Tara's pillared backdrop. For her part, Mitchell had fought the moviemakers on their plans to portray Tara as a mansion. In her imagination and her book, it had been a plain Georgia farmhouse. As she wrote to a journalist in February 1939, "'Tara' was very definitely not a white-columned mansion. I am mortally afraid the movies will depict it as a combination of the Grand Central Station, the old Capitol at Milledgeville and the Natchez houses of 'So Red the Rose.'"[58] She was, of course, right, and to this day *Gone with the Wind* exerts its seductive pull.

Throughout the thirties, forties, fifties, and beyond, white pillared imagery was heavily used for advertisements of southern products as diversified as gasoline, lumber, ham, and whiskey. Homes tours also glorified the region's antebellum architecture, beginning as early as 1932 in Natchez and spreading to other towns across the South.[59] As late as the spring of 1998, a travel writer for the *New York Times* demonstrated just how effectively authors, filmmakers, and advertisers had done their work when he described Natchez's historic homes as "that vast slumber party of antebellum Miss Havishams gathered on the high bank of the Mississippi River."[60]

THE HAMLIN THESIS AND STRANGER NOTIONS

Trained architectural historians had a better appreciation of the Greek Revival style's national reach. One scholar even went so far as to see its American popularity as a declaration of architectural independence from Europe, especially England. In his important book *Greek Revival Architecture in America* (1944), Talbot Hamlin stated a theory that stood for more than half a century. "The American Revolution brought a cultural as well as a political liberation," he wrote. "The whole country became at last architecturally free — and architecturally 'classic.' The colonial attitude was dead." According to Hamlin, antebellum Americans latched onto the architecture of ancient Athens as the highest embodiment of their own democratic ideals. This, he asserted, explained why the Greek Revival style spread so rapidly across the young republic.[61]

In the new millennium, historians revisited Hamlin and convincingly refuted his thesis. In his highly readable study *Architecture in the United States, 1800–1850* (2002), W. Barksdale Maynard delivered the coup de grâce. "Taste

Detail, Waring Texas on South Claiborne Street. Porches were nearly universal on Greek Revival buildings in the South, and Mobile's sultry air made them indispensable.

during these years was a truly international language," he wrote, "and the Greek Revival, far from being an American revolt against British cultural hegemony, was if anything an eager — one could almost say servile — acquiescence to foreign preferences."[62]

During the 1960s, some academics went Hamlin one better and argued that in the South the Greek Revival style was a psychic buttress to the slave order. Alan Gowans, a student of American material culture, declared "the Southern planter's columned mansion proclaimed his devotion to the hierarchical mores of an old-fashioned, almost feudal world."[63] In a 1977 lecture given at the University of Texas and subsequently published, architectural historian Robert Gamble took issue with this idea, stating that there was "little evidence that Southerners on the eve of the Civil War associated neoclassical architecture and the classic-style portico with the virtues of a peculiarly Southern way of life." Of more concern, he concluded, were "the price of cotton, sugar cane, or tobacco, the rise of the river, and the county election."[64] For their dwellings, they put up what was au courant, and that was Greek Revival.

THE NEW CLASSICISM

As the twentieth century drew to a close, a small but growing number of architects openly expressed their disenchantment with modern design and turned their talents to working in more traditional forms. In 1980 one architect asked, "Will we see a re-emergence of classical architecture? I suspect that we will. If a dentist did to your teeth what modern architecture has done to our cities, you would sue. Architects and the public at large are growing tired of the incoherence and shoddiness of much modern design, and classical architecture offers a security and coherence which many now seek."[65]

At least two American architectural schools — the University of Notre Dame and the University of Miami — have responded and now offer courses to satisfy a growing hunger for classical training among student architects. And The Institute of Classical Architecture and Classical America, which has as its charge "advancing the classical tradition in architecture," published a beautiful pattern book in 2007, providing precise drawings of the old orders just as Asher Benjamin and Minard Lafever did long ago. The institute has even forged a partnership with Habitat for Humanity to provide "affordable, classically-styled homes in historic districts" for lower-income residents.[66]

Two hundred years after Latrobe's Bank of Pennsylvania amazed passersby, the Greek Revival has reemerged with new examples of the style appearing across the nation, including in Mobile. Among the best of these is The News Building in Athens, Georgia, by Allan Greenberg. When William Morris III, the owner of a printing company and several small newspapers, commissioned this building, he remarked, "I couldn't build a glass palace in one of Georgia's great Classical cities." The architect Greenberg was proud of his handiwork and unapologetic about producing a neo-Grecian temple. He pointed to the base of one of the building's Ionic columns and quipped, "There's more architecture in that detail than in most new buildings."[67]

The story of Greek Revival Mobile mirrors this fascinating national saga, from the style's earliest nineteenth-century appearance to its contemporary re-emergence among a new breed of preservation architects. This absorbing story is filled with an engaging cast, whose architectural fruits still inspire aesthetic hearts.

CHAPTER ONE

PILLARED BEGINNINGS IN

ANTEBELLUM MOBILE

There was precious little classicism in early American Mobile. After a long century (1702–1813) of colonial rule by France, Britain, and then Spain, the town still only consisted of a few sandy streets hard by the Mobile River, a couple of wharves, a decaying brick fort, a rickety Catholic church, several dozen unimpressive one-story residences, and more graves in the unkempt cemetery than living citizens. The Americans brought new blood, energy, optimism, and soon enough, a passion for columns.

In 1820, shortly after Mobile's incorporation by the legislature of the brand-new state of Alabama, city fathers predicted bright prospects for their little "commercial emporium," announcing that "here a great city will arise."[1] Just two years later, the *Mobile Commercial Register* took stock of the growing community. There were, it proudly noted, nearly three thousand residents "of all colors" (roughly a third of whom were slaves or free blacks), living among 240 dwelling houses, 110 stores and warehouses, 2 churches, a post office, a custom house, a bank, "a building used as a court house," a jail, and "three commodious hotels." The paper was quick to admit that none of these buildings was particularly impressive. Most were built of wood, and "in many instances, the Spanish taste, as well as Spanish buildings, yet remain." The temporary courthouse was actually an unassuming rented cottage, and the jail was a laughingstock: "we shall only state, that it will contain prisoners in the day time, if well guarded." The hotels looked like nothing so much as oversized barns and, though possessed of a few amenities, were nonetheless "far short of those in some sections of the Union." About the only architecture worthy of the name was a small Protestant church then under construction, "the order somewhat of the Gothic." But according to the paper, better things loomed, as a new county courthouse "has been authorized, and arrangements are about to be made to commence it."[2]

A few months after the article ran, a design competition for the new courthouse was announced. Records do not reveal how many builders submitted plans, but the winners were a pair of New Englanders who had resided in the

Port City since Spanish times. Not much is known about Lewis Judson, who probably handled business and administrative matters for the partnership. But Peter Hobart clearly had a talent for architectural design that was perhaps influenced by buildings he had seen during his arduous journey down the eastern seaboard to the Gulf Coast twenty-five years earlier. He also possessed a good deal of civic and business experience. Still healthy in his forties, he was a Mason, a former night watchman, and a two-term city commissioner who had helped establish the young American boomtown's boundaries. In addition, he owned a profitable sawmill.[3]

The trappings of Hobart's working life as a builder/architect may be gleaned from his will, written on Christmas Eve 1827. Among his effects were a "desk, bookcase, books, maps, charts, drawing tools and instruments."[4] Though not enumerated in the will, the latter category likely included various pens and pencils, precision compasses, double rulers and T squares for drawing parallel lines, folding squares and protractors for rendering the many angles required, and perhaps some rudimentary survey equipment for laying out dimensions and measuring building sites. When Hobart died the following summer, the *Mobile Commercial Register* lauded him as a "fearless, upright and independent" citizen whose many labors had been "beneficial to the community."[5]

Hobart's drawings for the courthouse no longer survive, but the contract does, and it is detailed enough to allow a pretty good idea of the end result. For an overall cost of thirteen-thousand dollars Hobart and Judson erected a seventy-five-feet-long by fifty-feet-wide, two-story red brick structure on a raised foundation at the southwest corner of Government and Royal streets. The twelve-over-twelve pane, double-hung sash windows were accented by white marble sills and lintels (representing that stone's first local use), and the central entrance was distinguished by a heavy door with sidelights and a fan transom, typical of the earlier classicism. But the building's most significant feature was its monumental columned portico, the first ever in Alabama, with each of the four shafts fashioned of "brick and plaistered [sic] with Roman cement."[6] Unfortunately, the contract provides no clues to the order employed, but it was most likely Tuscan or, if the columns were fluted, Doric. Anything more elaborate, like the Ionic or Corinthian, would have almost certainly required further explication. Completed by 1828, the new Mobile County Courthouse represented a successful and elegant braiding of traditional elements with the emerging classical appetite. Sadly, Hobart didn't get to enjoy his legacy, but he had prepared the way, and it wasn't long before other builders followed suit.

The Greek Revival's conquest of Mobile was immeasurably helped by a catastrophic fire in the fall of 1827, which created a virtual blank slate of the downtown. It began during the wee hours Sunday morning, October 21, when flames appeared through the roof of the Mobile Hotel, located on Royal Street just north of Dauphin Street in the heart of the business quarter. Conditions were ripe for a rapid increase: a two-month drought with only one rain shower of note, water in short supply, and a strong northwest wind. Lastly, the number of citizens available to fight the fire was much reduced because of the prevailing fear of summer epidemics, which caused hundreds to abandon the city from May every year until the first killing frosts, usually late November.[7]

According to an account in the *Mobile Commercial Register*, nearby houses "caught with the quickness of powder," and soon all the buildings in the fire's widening path, "whether wooden or brick, fire proof or not, appeared to dissolve at its touch, without any more apparent resistance than if they had been columns of snow." By the time it was over, at least 169 structures "exclusive of warehouses and other back tenements not enumerated" had been destroyed in a nine-block area roughly bounded by Government Street to the south, St. Francis Street to the north, the Mobile River to the east, and St. Joseph Street to the west. Hobart and Judson's new courthouse was just beyond this zone and thus spared. The newspaper estimated losses at between a half million and a million dollars but concluded on a positive note, explaining that "the city, in all probability, will be rebuilt in less than two years, and will of course be better calculated to resist a similar visitation."[8] The first half of this statement proved correct; the second half, alas for the soon-to-be pillared city, did not.

Just as the paper had predicted, the ashes had barely cooled before Mobilians moved into the rubble to rebuild their city bigger and better than before. The press of business was such that practical structures were needed first if maximum profits were to be realized — wharves, warehouses, hostelries, shops, livery stables, offices, and coffeehouses (critical for impromptu wheeling and dealing). By the spring of 1832, one traveler marveled at the evident progress. Thomas Hamilton, a British writer touring the South from Charleston to New Orleans, knew about the recent blaze but could find few traces of it amid Mobile's commercial bustle. Despite his admiration for the rapid recovery, however, he was bothered by the residents' apparent lack of interest in anything but monetary pursuits. "Mobile is a place of trade, and nothing else," he wrote in a book published shortly after his return home. "There are no smart houses or equipages, nor indeed any demonstration of opulence, except huge warehouses and a crowded harbor. Of amusements of any kind, I heard nothing."[9] There was, of course, more to the picture, which Hamilton, during his brief passage, could not know.

The first years of the 1830s were, in fact, witness to the construction of three important structures — a college, a hospital, and a private residence — that effectively demonstrated Mobilians' broader concerns as well as their increasingly sophisticated grasp of how good architecture could influence the tone and perception of their growing community. By the time the last of these structures was underway in 1833, the Greek Revival could be said to have well and truly arrived, albeit with a Gulf Coast twist.

One of these buildings had actually been completed by the time of Hamilton's visit, but because it stood on the campus of Spring Hill College several miles west of downtown, few short-term visitors were aware of it. Founded in 1830 by Bishop Michael Portier, a French émigré, the college sat on an elevated site, well watered and timbered, with good roads nearby. It was part of Portier's overall plan to reinvigorate and solidify local Catholicism amid a burgeoning Protestant population. The Jesuit-staffed institution was a significant part of this endeavor, which also included a new cathedral, a girls' school, a hospital, and a cemetery.[10]

Portier's dreams were given attractive physical form by a talented young French cleric in his entourage named Claude Beroujon. Whether Beroujon had any formal architectural training is unknown, but he proved so adept at the craft that Portier turned to him again and again over the years. In the Spring Hill College building, completed by the spring of 1831, Beroujon unleashed his creative powers to the fullest, erecting a monumental three-story edifice with a pedimented, four-columned portico distinguished by an oval vent. The full-height Tuscan columns, in addition to making a strong architectural statement, also proved useful in supporting a series of balconies. The entrance featured a fanlight transom, while a delicate cupola with a clock capped off the structure.[11] In its employment of these elements, the Spring Hill building was, like the new courthouse downtown, still rooted in the older tradition, but Mobilians were clearly becoming enamored of columns on a grand scale. Shortly after the college's completion, a Jesuit wrote to his superior back in France: "You may think our colonnaded building an extravagance, but in hot climates galleries are an absolute necessity. Besides, this appearance of elegance and cleanliness was necessary in order to make a favorable impression on people who idolize their children and who place bodily comfort at the head of the list."[12] Locally then, classicism was proving itself to be a practical trend, formal yet easily adaptable to the area's climatic realities.

Two years later, closer in to town, yet another large colonnaded building was under construction, and though it too would owe something to colonial antecedents, in its massive scale and general heaviness it would stand as a forceful harbinger of the Greek Revival style, soon to dominate the Port City.

Mobile had had several hospitals during its colonial period. When the Americans arrived they used the old Spanish facility for a time, but soon arranged for a new one, which was erected in 1824.[13] Like so many of early American

Mobile's other buildings, however, this hospital was a thrown-together affair, small and undistinguished. Not surprisingly, it quickly proved inadequate to the needs of an expanding population exposed to the myriad medical risks of the early nineteenth century.

Alert to the matter, the board of aldermen met on April 17, 1833, and appointed a three-man committee "to acquire and purchase as soon as possible 6 acres of high and dry ground for the purpose of erecting a permanent City Hospital."[14] The committee selected a site at the corner of Broad and St. Anthony streets in the city's northwest quadrant, less than a mile and a half from the river.

By that summer city fathers were mulling over architectural plans, and they soon settled on a set submitted by Captain William George as "the most suitable, convenient and the cheapest."[15] Little is known about George, who is listed as a carpenter in the 1837 city directory. In all probability he was informally trained, like virtually everyone else plying the building trades in those days, but well connected and convincing enough to get a hearing. His involvement in the hospital project appears to have been limited, however, as after receiving seventy-five dollars for his drawings, he disappears from the records for the job.[16]

Not so the contractor, John K. Collins, who for the next three years managed the hospital's construction. Collins was a solid choice for this responsibility as he had been active in the local building trade for years, knew everybody (including Hobart, for whom he had served as executor), and could be depended upon to complete large projects. Still, in scope and complexity the hospital exceeded

Spring Hill College, from an 1865 view. The fourth story and side wings were added in 1859, and the entire structure burned to the ground a decade later. (Courtesy Spring Hill College Archives.)

The City Hospital as it appeared in 1912, shortly after the solid end bays were added. (Courtesy Erik Overbey Collection, University of South Alabama Archives.)

anything Collins had dealt with before, and his fee, a princely $34,000, reflected this. Good as that figure no doubt looked to him on paper, the realities of the job, including at least one unusual and unforeseen circumstance, cost him headaches aplenty. Some inkling of this is found in Collins's final bill, submitted to the mayor and aldermen in the winter of 1837. He reviewed his contract and complained that the aldermen had docked his pay for failure to complete the hospital on time. Collins explained that this delay had been unavoidable, because during a smallpox epidemic "the placing of persons suffering under an infectious disease in the building prevented me from procuring journeymen to work on it." He begged the aldermen to consider this and adjust his pay accordingly.[17]

Despite the difficulties and the wrangling, the finished product pleased everyone, including Mayor John Everett, who declared it "unsurpassed in beauty and architectural craftsmanship." Basking in the afterglow, he concluded, "The building with its classic Greek lines is as practical as it is beautiful."[18]

The mayor's enthusiasm was understandable. By any measure, the hospital was an important achievement for the hopeful young American town. Measuring 182 feet along St. Anthony Street by 65 feet deep, the building presented a colonnaded facade defined by a projecting five-bay, pedimented central block with wings of five bays to either side (in 1907, several solid bays were added at each end). Like the old Spring Hill College building, the hospital has balustraded galleries as well as a front door with a large fanlight (which originally displayed an eagle and arrow motif) and an oval vent (once glassed) in the pedimented gable above. Its interior layout is a simple central hall with a bisecting

The old City Hospital (1833–37) is still among the most imposing buildings downtown. The fanlight over the front entrance and the oval vent in the gable are more appropriate to an earlier phase of classicism, but the heavy colonnade completely overwhelms them and marks the structure as one of the earliest Gulf Coast examples of the Greek Revival.

James W. Roper, from a framed colored photograph of a miniature on ivory. (Courtesy Historic Mobile Preservation Society.)

transverse passage running the length of the building. Enfiladed chambers once served as offices, examination and operation rooms, and bedrooms.

More discerning eyes, and they were not long in appearing, would have recognized a lack of polish in certain aspects of the hospital's design. Though the fanlight and oval window are well rendered in the usual early, light classical fashion, these are minor elements completely overwhelmed by the building's robust colonnade. Here, George's amateur status is most clearly evident. At first glance, the Tuscan columns are certainly impressive to behold — thirty-two feet high, stucco-slathered brick complete with capitals and entasis. But closer inspection reveals the entasis to be clumsy, lacking the grace one associates with the Greek Revival style in pure form. Nonetheless, in the early 1830s the City Hospital represented the strongest expression of classicism yet in the Port City.

Even as Collins labored on the hospital at Broad Street, a Virginia transplant named James W. Roper embarked on constructing a personal residence a bit to the south and west that would eventually come to be recognized as one of the most beautiful and well-adapted Greek Revival houses in the nation.

Oakleigh is one of the most beautifully adapted Greek Revival residences in the South. Now a house museum, it draws approximately ten thousand visitors each year and is the site of a popular candlelight Christmas ceremony.

Oakleigh, from a ca. 1895 photograph by T. E. Armistead. The column capitals and perhaps the frieze appear to be painted a different color than the body of the house. Substantive changes to Oakleigh have been limited since its construction. (Courtesy T. E. Armistead Collection, University of South Alabama Archives.)

Nothing about James Roper would have indicated that he was about to produce that kind of architectural excellence, however. He came to Mobile in 1829 at age twenty-eight, married Sarah Ann Davenport, and lived in a small house downtown. He was hardly a wealthy man, owning just three slaves and a vacant lot, but he was skilled enough at a variety of endeavors, including the sale of flowering plants, cotton brokering, and brickmaking, that in just two years he purchased thirty-three acres of land on the city's western fringes.[19]

The site was within two miles of the all-important river yet well elevated at nearly thirty feet above sea level, was nicely timbered, and best of all, included an operational clay pit. It was the perfect place to live and, Roper no doubt believed, prosper. Sadly, his excitement was dealt a staggering blow in the spring of 1832, when twenty-two-year-old Sarah died in childbirth. Just six months later, their baby girl passed away as well. Roper's despair can only be imagined, as no correspondence or diaries survive, but he soon found ample and no doubt welcome distraction in the construction of his home, which he romantically christened Oakleigh, combining the name of the property's most common tree with an individualistic variation on the Anglo-Saxon word *lea*, for meadow.[20]

Roper designed the home himself and, over the next few years, harvested his own timber and clay for its construction, utilizing both slave and free labor. Though he made no claims to being an architect, Roper's deft blending of formal Greek Revival elements with traditional coastal building customs is stunning.

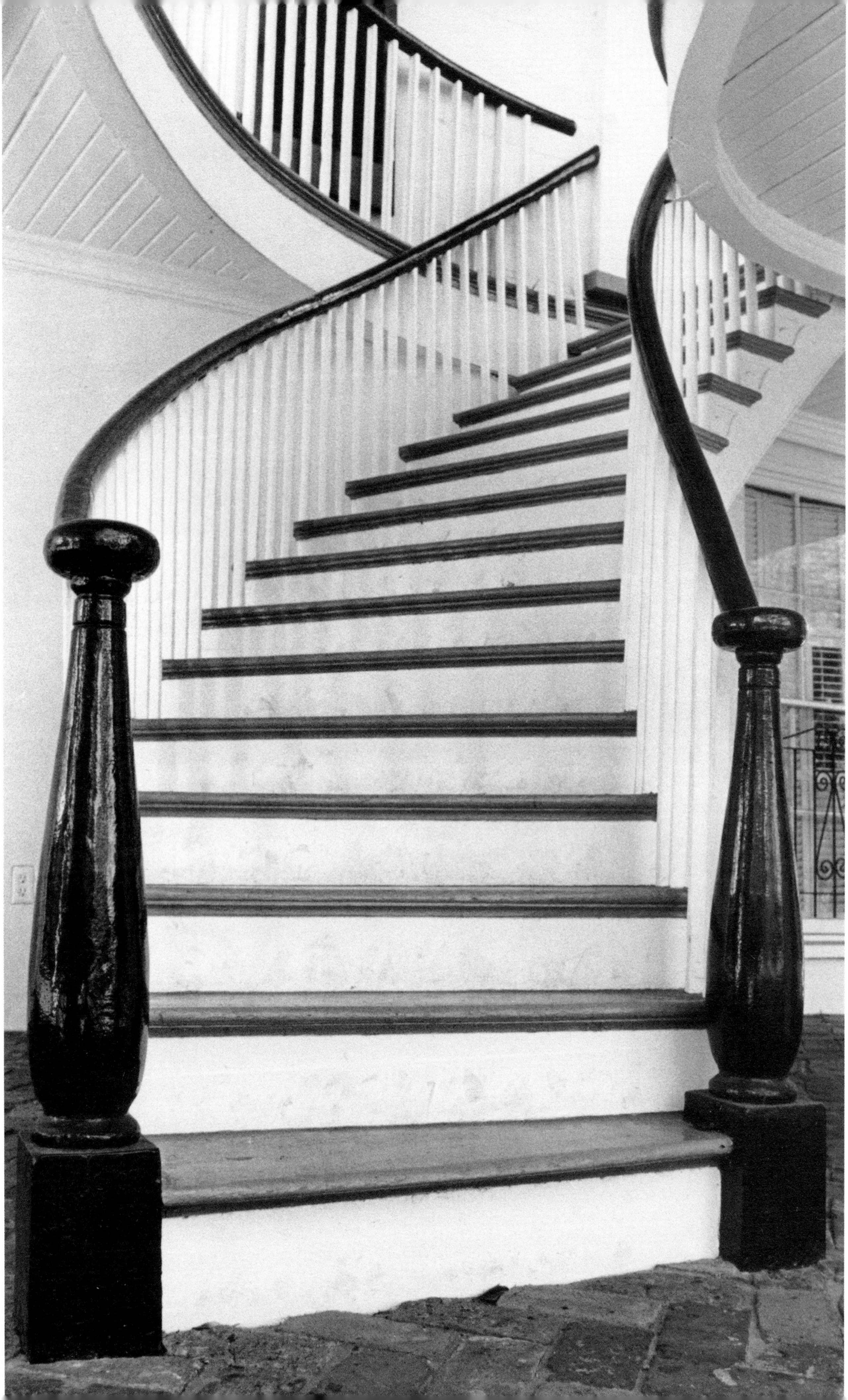

In form, plan, and execution, Oakleigh represents a wholly original and beautifully functional response to its locale. Facing east on its shaded knoll, the residence rests on a raised brick foundation, displaying boxed columns on its front and wing porches, a curved exterior stair punching through the main porch deck, and a low hip roof with a pedimented front gable. All in all, it is the very picture of semirural independence and elegance.

Roper's attentions to climatic realities include both large and small adjustments. To begin with, the home's T shape, with big sash windows along the sides and jibbed windows on the porches, provides cross-ventilation to every room. Interior circulation is further enhanced by the side-hall plan, high ceilings, double parlors with pocket doors, and traverse hall across the rear. The elevated foundation, since infilled but originally open with lattice panels between the piers, not only allowed for storing tools and larger knickknacks beneath the house but also admitted breezes. For those rare cold days on the Gulf Coast, fireplaces are present in every room.

By the time Oakleigh was finished in 1837, the tax value of Roper's parcel, which besides the house and the brick pit included a two-story kitchen and a

(Above) The view from Oakleigh's main porch is more country than city. At least two wedding proposals have occurred here, and among the notables who have visited are Augusta Evans Wilson, Mobile socialite Octavia LeVert, Henry Clay, Jefferson Davis, and James Garfield.

(Opposite) Oakleigh's curved exterior stair exhibits a high degree of workmanship.

First-floor plan, Oakleigh. Many of Mobile's Greek Revival houses employed the side-hall configuration.

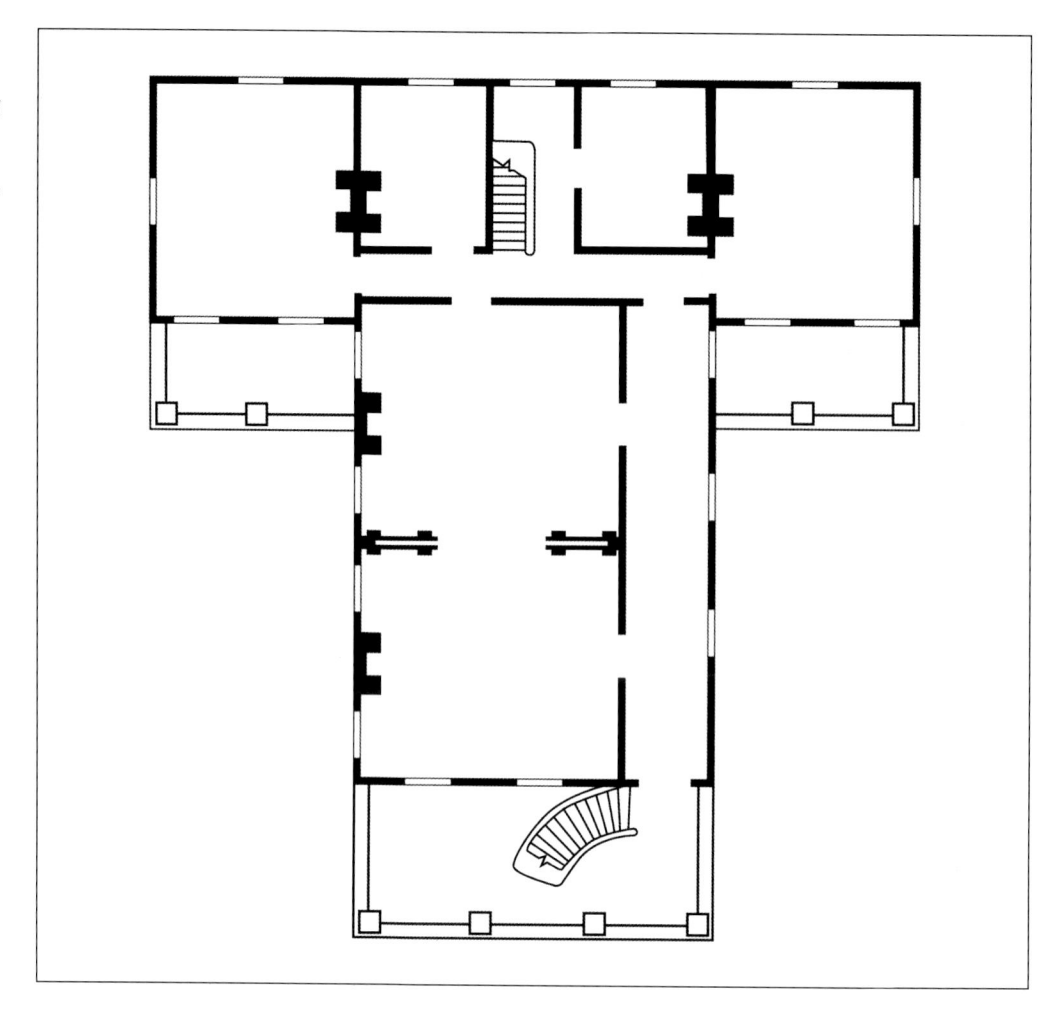

servants' quarter, had jumped from $2,500 to $25,000.[21] Things looked promising for him on other fronts as well. In 1836 he purchased a dry-goods store; increased the number of his slaves to eighteen, worth $16,000 (most of whom were working in his brickmaking operations at Oakleigh and downtown); and in the fall of 1838 he remarried.[22] His fortunes were rising as dramatically as those of his adopted city, but he had borrowed heavily to make it all happen, and any national economic downturn was likely to spell financial ruin.

The construction of Spring Hill College, the City Hospital, and Oakleigh was part of an economic surge transforming Alabama's only seaport. By any measure, Mobile's civic progress from the 1827 fire to the mid-1830s was impressive. Driven by the cotton-growing plantations upstate and in neighboring Mississippi, Mobile's importance as a commercial entrepôt increased dramatically. In 1830, just over one hundred thousand bales of cotton were exported from the city's wharves. By 1835 the figure was approaching two hundred thousand bales.[23] The price per pound of cotton rose right along — from nine cents to fourteen cents per pound.[24] The value of the city's imports increased

Side-hall entrance, Oakleigh. The transom and eared architrave door surround are typical of the period. The marble-top table to the left features a so-called petticoat mirror. In actuality, the mirror was meant to reflect light and rug patterns, as it is impossible to see the hem of a dress when standing before it.

Oakleigh's grand double parlors have delighted tourists for more than forty years. The furnishings are not original to the house, but none would have been out of place during Roper's tenure. The original lighting was by whale oil, later converted to gas and then electricity.

as well, from $144,823 in 1830 to over half a million dollars five years later.[25] The export-import imbalance was stark, but few worried about it amid the good news. Mostly cotton, and some timber, was shipped out, while just about everything else necessary to nineteenth-century civilized living — china, silver, crystal, hardware, literature, artwork, furniture, pianos, and fashionable hats, gloves, shoes, and dresses — had to be imported.

In 1833, the *Mobile Register* was delighted by the trends. "Six years ago," it editorialized, "this city of Mobile was reduced to ashes, by a dreadful conflagration — it has since risen in all the vigor and beauty of a phoenix."[26] City fathers attempted to keep abreast of development, cutting new roads and improving drainage. In the fall of 1833, Spring Hill Avenue was widened to sixty feet, pushed out to "the forks of the Springhill and St. Stephens Roads," and covered with oyster shells, all to the tune of $2,900.[27]

Everywhere one looked, there was activity, and outsiders started to take notice. In November 1835, a Boston newspaper reprinted for its readers a Mobile reporter's account. "In every direction the eye meets buildings going up," the anonymous newspaperman wrote, "and other improvements progressing. It is computed that since last season upwards of fifty new stores, and more than one hundred dwellings, have been and are now being erected." More buildings meant more people. "The increase of population," the reporter continued, "it is thought, will be at least 2000; many of whom squeeze themselves into the already crowded hotels."[28]

Melissa Russell, the sister of an Indian agent from Massachusetts, came down to visit her brother in 1835 and was astonished by all the construction projects underway. "It is a growing city, certainly," she wrote, "for every street is filled with lumber and bricks for building new or altering old blocks."[29] In the spring of 1836, another visitor counted three hundred new stores and residences erected over the last year. The city's waterfront was equally vibrant. "No less than 4,000 seamen were employed in the trade of Mobile last season," this visitor explained, and fifty sailing ships then in the harbor made the figure believable.[30]

Those ships brought passengers as well as cargo, and among the throng streaming into Mobile during these years was a pair of young architects (soon to be joined by a third) fresh out of New York City, well versed in their trade and bent on making their mark in a new place. Their original destination was New Orleans, but word of a yellow fever epidemic there caused them to lay over in Mobile. While in the Port City, they met one of the most remarkable businessmen in Alabama history, and the resulting alliance was to lift Mobile architecture from the parochial into the realm of the first-rate.

James Gallier had been frustrated with his "horse in a mill routine" in New York's competitive building market, and young Charles Dakin was eager to establish himself and make more money. Together, the two men decided to strike out for the Gulf Coast, lured by reports of large construction projects there and a dearth of trained professionals to plan and oversee them. They were cognizant of the health risks posed by the area's subtropical climate, but Gallier decided to "run the hazard" anyhow, albeit with his wife and small child left safely ensconced in New York.[31]

After waiting out the epidemic in Mobile, during which time they likely designed Barton Academy and Government Street Presbyterian Church, Gallier and Dakin made the short hop over to the Crescent City, where, Gallier recalled in his autobiography, they "hired an office on Canal St., hung its walls with plans and drawings, and began to look out for something to do."[32] They were soon busier than they could have imagined, erecting row houses, an Episcopal

James Gallier, from an 1838 portrait. (Courtesy Louisiana State Museum.)

Henry Hitchcock, from a painting. (Courtesy Erik Overbey Collection, University of South Alabama Archives.)

church, stores, warehouses, and an arcade, all in the Greek Revival style.[33] Business was so good that Charles's older brother, James, soon joined them, arriving by steamboat in November 1835. Even as the three men were reunited in New Orleans, however, the possibilities offered by the frenzied building activity in nearby Mobile attracted them, and on New Year's Eve Charles returned to the Alabama seaport to open a branch office.[34]

Exactly when these ambitious builders made the acquaintance of businessman Henry Hitchcock is uncertain, but it was probably in the fall of 1834 when they first landed or shortly thereafter. In his autobiography, Gallier described a design competition that he and Charles Dakin entered for a new Mobile City Hall (never built). Their drawings "obtained the first prize of three hundred dollars," Gallier wrote, "though but a trifle, it served to place our names before the public."[35] Given Hitchcock's local prominence in commercial, political, and legal circles, he likely would have met the architects during this competition. In any case, Hitchcock proved to be an architect's dream — well heeled and connected, easy to work with, and attuned to the importance of good design to larger civic aspirations.

Hitchcock was born in Vermont in 1795. He was a grandson of the Revolutionary War hero Ethan Allen but was cynical about the association, once remarking that nothing of any substance had ever come his way from it. He came to the Tombigbee district of the Alabama Territory in 1817 and began the practice of law. The following year Governor William Bibb appointed him territorial secretary. Hitchcock's involvement in state politics included helping prepare the state constitution and a stint as attorney general from 1819 to 1823. During his tenure at that post, he authored the first book to be published in the new state, *Alabama Justice of the Peace* (1822) and, on the domestic front, married Anna Erwin, who proved a loving, sympathetic, and supportive partner, in 1821. Hitchcock moved to Mobile in 1826 and served as a U.S. district attorney before his election to the state Supreme Court in 1835. By that time, he and his wife had two young sons and a daughter.[36]

In addition to his legal and political work, Hitchcock was a bona fide Maecenas, vitally interested in his adopted city's development across a wide spectrum — business, the arts, education, religion — and busied himself advancing as many of these endeavors as he could. He had a great deal of capital and held an interest in such enterprises as the Mobile Acqueduct Company and the Mobile Steam Cotton Press and Building Company. Happily for Gallier and the Dakins, not to mention uncounted local tradesmen, all of this translated into lots of construction. In 1835 alone, Hitchcock erected sixteen brick buildings, all of them three and four stories.[37]

Mobile's extraordinary architectural flowering of the late 1830s depended not only on the merging of Hitchcock's money with Gallier and the Dakins' design talent but upon the availability of competent, skilled craftsmen in all the building trades. Easy access to good raw materials and quality construction supplies was also important. Fortunately, everything needed was already well in place by the time the Vermont millionaire and the New York architects cemented their relationship.

As early as 1822, the *Mobile Commercial Register* remarked that "the common branches of mechanism are tolerably numerous."[38] After the 1827 fire, the opportunities for skilled and even unskilled builders exploded. Wages followed suit — a good carpenter could command five dollars a day, a handsome sum for the early nineteenth century.[39] Despite the abundance of high-paying construction work, antebellum Mobile suffered frequent and perplexing labor shortages.[40] The upshot was that the best workers could count on steady and lucrative employment.

For those carpenters with a desire to master the intricacies of the emerging Greek Revival style and thereby improve their prospects even more, printed information was readily available to help them. By the mid-1830s, pattern books were for sale locally within weeks of printing, including Chester Hill's *The Builder's Guide*, which touted itself as "a practical treatise on the several orders of Grecian and Roman architecture, together with the Gothic style of building." The profusely illustrated volume included tutorials on joinery, masonry, and sculpture. J. S. Kellogg and Co., the local merchant offering the guide, invited Port City mechanics "to call and examine it."[41]

Who were these men whose physical strength, dexterity, and love of craft made Mobile's Greek Revival buildings possible? To begin with, like Hobart, Portier, Beroujon, Roper, Hitchcock, and almost everyone else in town, they were from someplace else. They arrived throughout the antebellum period, bringing their hopes and skills from the eastern seaboard, the Midwest, and Europe, attracted by Mobile's international reputation as a busy seaport. These ambitious young men included Levi Conigle, a Polish painter; Daniel Cronin, an Irish stonecutter; Louis Dare, a Swiss cabinetmaker; C. Julian Gregral, a German plasterer; John Horn, an English mason; John Cortright, a New Jersey carpenter; and Freeman P. Creary, an Ohio brickmaker.[42]

They lived wherever they could find affordable lodgings, and at least two Dauphin Street establishments, Mechanics House and Mechanics Retreat, catered exclusively to members of the building trades. For amusement, they frequented the horse track, coffee saloons, oyster bars, whorehouses, and gambling dens, smoking cigars and trying their luck at love or roulette, faro, and keno.[43]

PLASTERING.
PETER RIACH,

No. Burden's Row, St. Francis Street,

Informs the citizens of Mobile that he is in readiness to execute orders in the above line of business with despatch, and will be thankful for a share of patronage.

R. R. DADE, Printer.

(Above) Peter Riach was one of many local tradesmen who advertised his services. His birthplace is unknown. From City of Mobile Directory, *1839.*

(Right) Advertisement for Mechanics Retreat from City of Mobile Directory, *1839.*

MOBILE DIRECTORY. 77

MECHANICS RETREAT,

By CHARLES BERG,
Corner of Franklin & Dauphin Streets.

The Bar is supplied with choice Liquors, and attached to which are conveniencies for the exercise and amusement of his customers.

☞ Boarders and strangers can be accommodated by the day, week, month, or year, on reasonable terms.

When at work, they were fortunate that local ordinances offered at least a modicum of protection for their efforts. Beginning in 1839 and culminating in 1841, the city passed a series of measures meant to regulate the trade. "An Act for the better securing Mechanics in the City and County of Mobile" provided that any "journeyman, laborer, cartman, sub-contractor or otherwise" who had not been paid for materials or labor could seek restitution from the building owner, who was then empowered to deduct the amount from the contractor's overall fee. The ordinance also provided for arbitration to resolve any disagreements between the contractor and "his journeyman or other person" as to the worth of the materials or the services rendered.[44]

Nice as it was to function within a legal framework, Mobile's tradesmen were also active on their own account. In fraternal common cause they formed groups like the Mobile Carpentry and Joiners' Mutual Benefit Society, which besides addressing professional and technical issues, offered a valuable social outlet. Like most other white male citizens in town, these tradesmen also belonged to Masonic groups and served in militia and fire companies, which allowed them to come into contact with a broader spectrum of society than might have otherwise been the case.[45]

Skilled artisan slaves and free blacks also contributed to Mobile's physical development. The number of free blacks was especially large for a southern city — more than eight hundred by 1850, working at a variety of occupations. Among these were thirty-one carpenters, five bricklayers, three painters, and one plasterer. At least four free black men in construction — carpenters Joseph Lorant, John Trenier Sr., and Edward Pollard, and bricklayer Noel Fornia — owned property worth more than one thousand dollars in 1850, a good indicator of both their ability and the local opportunities, even for a disadvantaged and increasingly oppressed group.[46]

For skilled white artisans, unconstrained by the legal and social limitations free blacks and slaves faced, the possibilities were even greater. As Gallier had noted upon his arrival in New York City in 1832, building contractors were not above calling themselves architects, based on no training whatsoever but rather on a desire to rise in the trades and make more money. Hebron Palmer, a draftsman who had worked in New York and then relocated to Mobile in the early 1830s, followed this pattern. He enthused in a letter to Alexander Jackson Davis: "Architectural talent is well appreciated and rewarded. I have a bank which is to be the best in the United States [and] a church now underway." Palmer may also have done drafting work for the Dakins in Mobile, which certainly would have been an education in good design and proper proportions. In any case, by 1837 he was calling himself an architect, one of a mere handful at that early date claiming the title.[47]

Others quickly imitated Palmer's example. Thomas Ellison Jr. was listed as a carpenter in the 1837 and 1838 city directories, but the next year he was listed as an architect. Cary W. Butt, who appears to have gotten his start drawing for the Dakins, called himself an "architect and builder" beginning in 1837. Others took a little longer to make the transition. William Alderson was an iron and brass founder through the 1840s, but by 1852 he labeled himself an architect also.[48]

There were undoubtedly a few posers and charlatans in the lot, but many had a genuine gift for the art, and their determination to improve their skills and opportunities was unbounded. One of the most interesting of these self-made architects was Thomas S. James, a Virginia native who at age thirty came to Mobile in 1835. He married a local woman named Laura Spalding Bell and went to work as a builder and bricklayer. James could be both gentle and abrasive. He had a reputation as something of an aesthete who loved arranging flowers and playing his Stradivarius violin, but he was sometimes harsh and opinionated, as demonstrated in his uncompromising Unionist sentiments when the Civil War approached. These were to cost him his life.[49]

Like some of his colleagues, James had been listed as a builder through the 1830s and 1840s, but by 1852 he assumed the mantle of architect.[50] His reliability and excellent workmanship paid off to such an extent that by 1860 the value of his personal estate was five thousand dollars.[51] As a supplement to his income, James opened a door, sash, and blind business, and even advertised his services upstate, which like Mobile was experiencing a Greek Revival building boom. In an ad in the *Marengo County Directory* for 1860, James listed among his products "Wood mouldings, of various patterns, Brackets, Consoles, Trusses, Mahogany Plank, Balusters, Newels, Stair railing, &C."[52] At home in

Thomas S. and Laura Bell James strike a grim pose in this ca. 1860 photograph. Thomas looks worn and unhealthy after decades as a builder/architect. Shortly after this picture was taken, he was throttled for his strident Unionism. (Courtesy of the Museum of Mobile.)

Mobile, James solicited architectural work, offering "drawings, specifications, estimates" and vowing that he was "determined to make our business a blessing to every man that favors us with his patronage."[53]

James proved adroit at forging relationships with other tradesmen and often contracted with them on complicated jobs, just as Gallier did on New Orleans's St. Charles Hotel. In the winter of 1838, he worked closely with Robert R. Walker and T. C. Nodine, a pair of master carpenters, on a contract "to erect pillars and a chimney" on a Dauphin Street building.[54] There is also at least one recorded instance of his using the services of a slave, though given the scale of his projects he must have done this frequently. In early 1857 James confirmed a slave owner's seventy-four dollar bill to the city for "work done by boy 'Mike'" over a thirty-two-day period.[55] This was when James was building the new Italianate-style City Hall and likely reflects the fairly common antebellum practice of owners hiring out their slaves to civilian contractors or governmental authorities. For slave owners, it was a handy way to realize cash money for their chattels' labors, especially during otherwise idle times around the house or farm.[56]

Mobile's builders enjoyed easy access to abundant raw materials. Clay veins around the bay had supported brickmaking and pottery operations since the early eighteenth century, and numerous sawmills exploited the surrounding thick forests, which were rich in cypress, longleaf pine, oak, and poplar, all superior construction woods.

Between 1819 and 1831, Eleazer Phillips and James Gourlay ran a brickyard on the Dog River, just south of the city limits, and of course Roper was soon successfully doing the same alongside Oakleigh. There was nothing quiet or subtle in the day-to-day doings of a large brickyard. Laborers dug out the clay, ground it, tamped it into wooden molds, and then shoved the molds into kilns for firing.[57] Shouts, ax thuds, fire, smoke, dust, mud, and the constant rumble and rattle of wagons and drays made clay pits undesirable where people lived and worked. City fathers recognized this, and in 1848 restricted such endeavors within the city limits. Exceptions were made for those landowners who obtained written permission "from two-thirds of the citizens living nearest to the place of location of said contemplated brick yard." In such an eventuality, the mayor could issue a license "to run for one year."[58] Despite this regulation, there were enough clay pits within easy traveling distance of downtown that builders felt no adverse effects.

Equally important was good lumber, which was more than adequately supplied by area sawmills. Hobart himself owned one such mill fourteen miles southwest of the city center, but a nearby waterway allowed him to raft lumber into town within a day's time. By 1835 John J. Deshon had one of the largest sawmills on the Gulf Coast going full capacity. He used an eighty-horsepower steam engine to run thirty-six saws, all connected to a single ninety-foot-long shaft. Deshon's mill employed both whites and blacks, though only whites got to do the skilled work. The mill produced twenty thousand board feet of lumber per day, and smaller saws turned out laths and shingles. Active sawmills were just as objectionable as brickyards within the city, of course, but lumberyards were not, and throughout the antebellum period large quantities of wood were rafted or hauled into these marshaling areas, most of them along the river, where builders could inspect and purchase what they needed. In 1852 one such yard had over a million board feet of lumber stacked within its confines, and a year later another had 150,000 shingles available.[59]

What with all the construction, these lumberyards were busy places, and authorities made sure their attendant activities did not unduly damage public property. In the fall of 1834, city officials passed an ordinance protecting the downtown streets from anyone attempting to drag their lumber along the ground. There had apparently been problems with the ends of long boards or logs dangling off wagons or carts and churning up the soil. Those who ignored the new rule were subject to a small fine.[60]

More finished products were obtainable as well. Besides James's sash and door outfit, there were several others, including one Beroujon established as early as 1839. Here builders could buy prefabricated architectural elements for a fraction of what they would have to pay a carpenter or joiner to craft them onsite. There were also hardware stores that supplied all kinds of locks, hinges, kickplates, firebacks, shutter dogs, and light fixtures; stonecutters who sold marble mantels and thresholds; painters who could do quality interior marbling and graining; and for the homeowner ready to move into his completed Greek Revival house, furniture stores that stocked sideboards, beds, sofas, wardrobes, secretaries, pier tables, dining tables, and chairs of all sorts.[61]

Thus, when Charles Dakin stepped ashore on that long-ago moonlit New Year's Eve, he no doubt felt optimistic about the prospects of doing serious architecture in Mobile, Alabama. The signs of a confident and vibrant city were all around him. The wharf was hedged by six steamboats, three schooners, and a ship, while a brig loaded with cotton, lumber, and pitch rocked gently midriver. The steamboat *Choctaw* had just chugged into port carrying 766 bales of Black Belt cotton. Sailors caroused in the bars and brothels, while more refined citizens sampled two plays staged that night, *All in the Wrong* and *Sprigs of Laurel*. Pallets of fresh-made brick were stacked along the gas-lit sidewalks, inconveniencing pedestrians, and piles of newly sawn lumber scented the air. Soft yellow light twinkled from dozens of windowpanes, and wood smoke curled upward from a thousand chimneys. There was money everywhere, and as he shouldered his bags, in one of which was stuffed a well-thumbed copy of *The Beauties of Modern Architecture*, young Dakin must have been exhilarated by the thought that there was nothing in the pattern book, or in his fertile imagination, that the people of his adopted city could not make real in three dimensions.[62]

CHAPTER TWO

PILLARED CITY,

PILLARED RUIN,

1836–1839

The latter half of the 1830s was a period of extraordinary activity and consequence in Mobile's architectural history. So much happened so fast that sorting it all out and presenting it in coherent fashion poses a challenge. Two of the city's most important landmark Greek Revival structures were begun on the very same day in 1836, and two others followed suit within months, as did numerous smaller ones, all under Charles Dakin's apparently indefatigable supervision (his brother and Gallier mostly offered design assistance). That one architect of his callow years could competently oversee this many overlapping jobs with the attendant logistical, technical, and personnel issues boggles the mind. Nor was Dakin the only builder/architect working up to his fullest potential during these years. Thomas S. James, Cary Butt, Hebron Palmer, and many others were all productive, so much so that by decade's end, their labors had well and truly transformed Mobile from rude shantytown into grand pillared city. It must have seemed a miracle at the time. Unfortunately, before the last coat of paint began to dry on the columned rotunda of the United States Hotel, the triple blows of bankruptcy, epidemic, and fire brought chaos, ruin, and despair.

But at first there was only exciting possibility. Within a few weeks of his arrival in late 1835, Charles Dakin inked a previously negotiated partnership deal with his brother James and established an office on Conception Street downtown, between St. Louis and St. Michael streets. Even though James was the better-known figure, the firm went by the name C. B. Dakin and Brother. The elder Dakin shuttled between New Orleans and Mobile a great deal during these months, but his younger sibling clearly bore the responsibility for day-to-day operations and stood to gain the most credit if things went well. Charles Dakin's evident involvement through the entire building cycle — from conception and design through construction — was somewhat unusual for the 1830s, when architects usually just supplied drawings, sometimes without signing them, and then moved on while contractors oversaw the job (and often referred to themselves as "architects" in the process). Gallier, who was by then fully engaged in New Orleans, played a lesser role, though he undoubtedly contributed significantly to the design of Government Street Presbyterian Church and Barton Academy, both of which he mentions in his autobiography.[1]

These buildings are among the most important ever constructed in Mobile, and they still stand on busy Government Street, their columns framed by live oaks. Henry Hitchcock was directly responsible for both of them. The church was born of his deep-seated desire to provide a handsome home for his newfound faith, and the school from his sincere belief in education and its importance to any civilized community. It was he who provided the drive and, to a considerable degree, the wherewithal to make each of these buildings a reality. Writing nearly thirty years afterward, Gallier did not exaggerate when he declared them "still the most important-looking buildings in Government Street."[2] And so they remain to this day.

Despite his happy marriage and considerable business success, Hitchcock was spiritually troubled, as he eventually admitted to Rev. William Hamilton, a Presbyterian minister and former New Jersey resident who was sent to Mobile in the fall of 1834. Upon his arrival, Hamilton boarded with the Hitchcock family for a time, during which he and his hosts became quite well acquainted. Several years later, Hamilton recalled that Hitchcock was known to be "strongly opposed to warm hearted piety, and especially to all religious excitement," and the minister thus thought it prudent to avoid the subject. Soon enough, however, the barriers came down, and in a series of conversations, Hitchcock poured out his feelings. According to Hamilton, he finally burst into tears and admitted that his greatest shortcoming was his "pride of character! my heart is too proud to submit to be saved, like the notorious sinner, by the righteousness of another; and . . . if God does not freely extend his mercy to me, and change my proud heart, — I am lost." The astonished reverend counseled the distraught lawyer, who after a period of reflection and prayer, accepted Jesus Christ and made a public profession in church, "falling on his knees, in broken tones, and with tears."[3]

The church where Hitchcock announced his conversion was a humble edifice. Presbyterians were as yet a tiny presence in the Port City. In 1821 the Presbytery of Alabama had organized with only three churches and fifty members. In Mobile their numbers were so small that they formed a union church with the Episcopalians. By 1828 they had unofficially established themselves under Rev. Murdock Murphy as the Presbyterian Church on Government Street and met in a frame building. Three years later, they formally organized, and three years after that Rev. Hamilton arrived. Meanwhile, their numbers were growing, though the congregation still amounted to fewer than two hundred souls.[4]

These were, however, people of social standing and influence, and they couldn't have been more fortunate in landing Henry Hitchcock as their newest committed and conscientious member. In the spring of 1835, Hitchcock, now a judge and acting as a trustee, bought a large square lot at the northwest corner of Government and Jackson streets for a new sanctuary, and together with the contractor John K. Collins, who was still at work on the City Hospital, set up a building committee. It was undoubtedly Hitchcock who secured Gallier and Dakin for the design, perhaps as early as the fall of 1834. In December 1835 the following ad ran in the *Mobile Commercial Register*:

> separate proposals from carpenters and masons for building a Presbyterian Church . . . will be received by the Building Committee until the 24th of December next. The carpenter's proposals will embrace the covering of the roof, and all the carpenters, jointers, builders, glaziers and plumbers work. The mason's proposals will embrace the excavations for the foundations, and all the brick, plasterers and stone cutters work, and also a proper stage all around the exterior of the building, the work to be entirely completed by the first of October next. The specifications and drawings can be seen at the office of the Mobile Steam Cotton Press and Building.[5]

That drawings and specifications were available indicates that Charles Dakin and Gallier had indeed already consulted with Hitchcock and done design work for the building in their New Orleans office prior to Charles's opening the branch office.

Two brothers, Robert and James Barnes, won the carpentry contract, while Thomas James got the masonry work. The latter amounted to more than forty thousand dollars of the sixty-thousand-dollar total construction cost, hardly a surprise given that the building is mostly stuccoed brick with stone front steps. James was lucky in that he could acquire the many thousands of needed bricks locally. Not so the more complicated stonework, which had to be custom cut and shipped from up north. This was also the case with the more involved joinery work, which the Barnes brothers had to arrange. Such long-distance shipping could be troublesome if there were delays or mix-ups with the order, necessitating weeks to untangle. But records indicate that the imported work for the church arrived pretty steadily — granite for the steps aboard the brig *Comet* on September 26, 1836, and "joiners work" about six weeks later aboard the ship *St. John*. In the scheme of things it was a minor inconvenience. Even in neighboring New Orleans, larger and home to more tradesmen, Gallier had to import materials and elements for the St. Charles Hotel job.[6]

(Opposite) Government Street Presbyterian Church is Mobile's most perfect Greek Revival building. The congregation has remained vibrant and prides itself on loving and historically sensitive stewardship of the structure.

Construction began on the church February 13, 1836. Dakin must have found Mobile's soft, sandy clay loam a luxury to excavate, when back home in New York the ground was likely still frozen. He must also have appreciated the fact that experienced men like Thomas James required relatively little supervision, freeing Dakin to solve problems (and they were many) on his other projects. Surely whenever he paused at the corner of Government and Jackson, he admired James's gangs of masons strung along the steadily rising scaffolding, throwing down their brick at breathtaking speed.

Despite the masons' competence, the projected October completion date went unmet, but no one complained, and Hitchcock, Hamilton, Dakin, and the congregation were obviously pleased with the progress. By March 1837, the rear wall was topped off and the finishing touches put on the front steps. The church was presentable enough inside and out for Charles Dakin to be married there on March 22, 1837, to Caroline Webb, a widow and the younger sister of James Dakin's wife.[7] Two days later the session minutes referenced the "new and commodious edifice" as nearly ready for "public worship."[8] On June 1, the newspaper announced that pews were being rented, and praised the finished building as "an ornament to the city."[9]

Today Government Street Presbyterian Church is one of two National Historic Landmarks in the city of Mobile, a designation reserved for buildings and sites of the highest importance. It is so recognized not only as an intact example of the distyle in antis formula perfected by Town and Davis in their New York designs (especially that of the Washington Street Methodist Episcopal Church, 1832, of which Government Street Presbyterian Church is a virtual copy), but furthermore as a rare survivor and the forerunner of others of the type locally and in the South, like Christ Church, Charleston's Temple Beth Elohim (1841), and Richmond's St. Paul's Church (1845).[10]

The building is one story over a raised basement, with a gable roof to the street. Before its rear additions (1905 and 1916), it measured 68 by 100 feet. The facade is distinguished by the distyle in antis configuration, featuring Ionic columns with flanking pilasters for two bays to either side. Of note are the entrance doors, which include rectangular panels above to compensate for the monumentality of the facade. The double doors are paneled wood. The side bays are divided by pilasters, making the church a pilastraded building, and display full-height Davisean windows (originally clear glass triple-hung sash but in 1905 converted to stained glass). The full entablature features denticulation along the cornice, and the front and rear gables are pedimented. The original antefixae are no longer present. Nor is the two-step, battered octagonal tower, blown down in an 1852 storm and never replaced.[11]

The interior presents a stunning display of chaste Protestant elegance. There

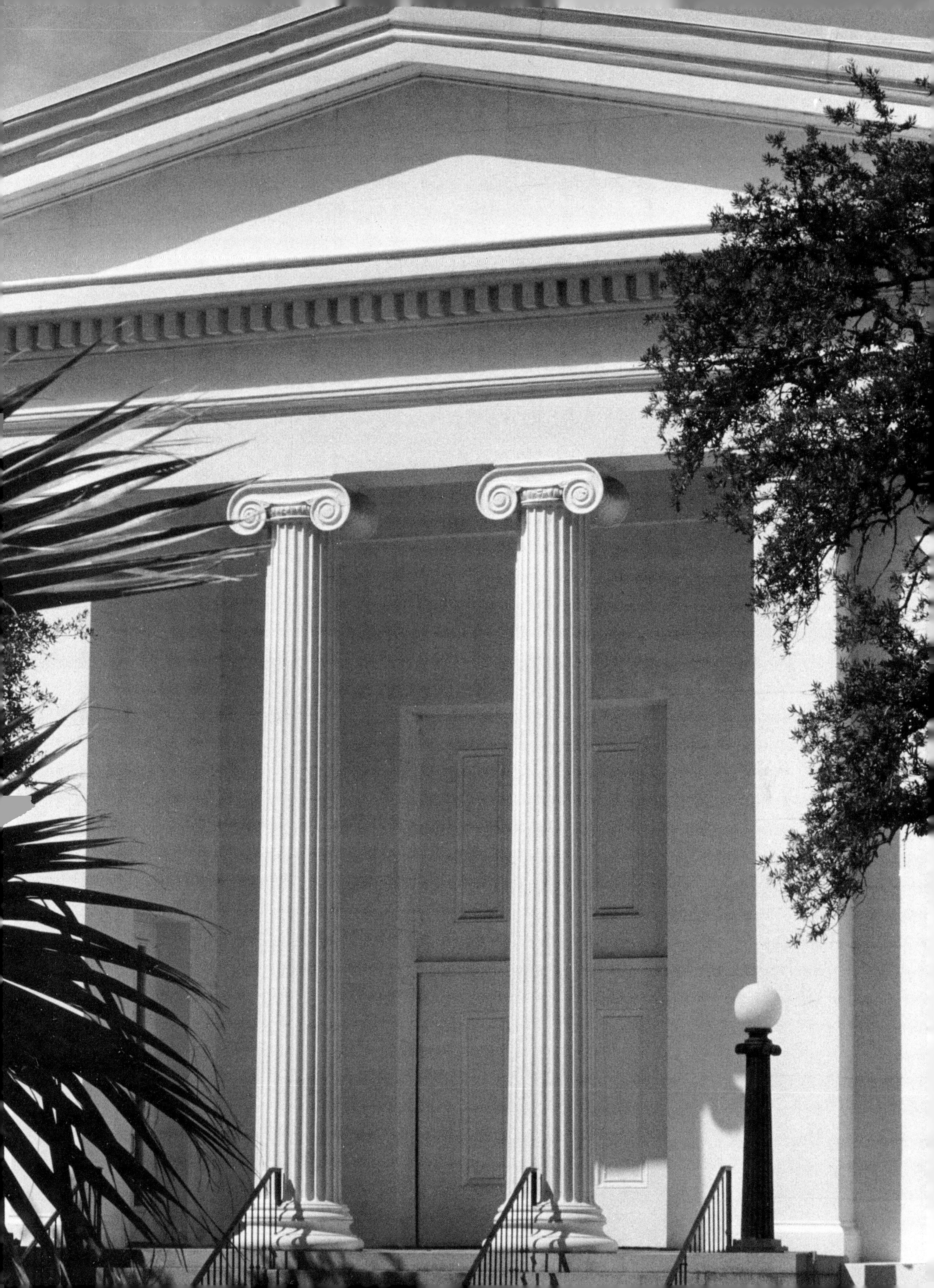

Detail, Government Street Presbyterian Church's distyle in antis Ionic facade. One prominent architectural historian recently dubbed this building one of the most beautiful Greek Revival churches in the nation.

are three entrances from the portico into the sanctuary. The main double doors lead directly inside, while double glass and wood doors open into the side vestibules. Curved staircases run from basement to gallery in each vestibule. The sanctuary itself is an open plan with two aisles. Pews are original, but their quaint side doors were removed more than a century ago. A U-shaped gallery

Government Street's paneled entrance doors are sheltered by the deep porch and soaring Ionic columns.

wraps around the interior and is supported on fluted columns, copied directly from plate 48 of Lafever's *The Beauties of Modern Architecture*. The large dais (with pulpit) dates from about 1893. Documentary evidence suggests that the first dais was similar in materials and dimensions to this replacement. Behind the altar a pylonlike structure frames an engaged Corinthian tetrastyle topped by anthemion cresting (the columns and cresting are from Lafever, plates 43 and 44, and as on the Choragic Monument of Lysicrates). Interior walls are plastered, and a full entablature meets the ceiling, featuring rosettes and denticulation. The interior's standout feature, however, is the plastered, coffered ceiling. The diamond-shaped coffers with their beaded borders are exquisitely constructed and must have elicited audible gasps when first glimpsed by the congregation.

Architectural historians have long attempted to guess who designed exactly which part of the church, but in the end it remains a parlor game. The building obviously owes much to the Town and Davis school, which had nourished Gallier and both Dakins. The consensus opinion is that Gallier and Charles Dakin designed the exterior, whereas the Dakin brothers are due credit for the

Interior, Government Street Presbyterian Church. The spectacular coffered ceiling, gallery, and monumental screen with its four Corinthian columns all helped qualify this building for National Historic Landmark status in 1994.

spectacular interior.[12] Whatever the case, the church set a new design standard for the Port City, one rarely exceeded or even met since.

Just four blocks to the west of the church, construction began on Barton Academy February 13, 1836, also. Like the church, Barton is a commanding example of the Greek Revival style and in its day represented a further degree of maturation for the rowdy seaport. Unfortunately, it hasn't been as lovingly cared for as some of Mobile's other historic treasures.

Schooling in early American Mobile was uneven and far from universal. Small private academies and female seminaries were available for those who could afford them, but there was nothing resembling public education. Recognizing the need, Mobile's state representative, Willoughby Barton, introduced a bill to create a local Board of School Commissioners, which passed on January 10, 1826. Shortly thereafter, two dozen leading citizens, including Peter Hobart and Henry Hitchcock, took their places on the board.[13]

The dream of public education wasn't easily realized, however. The board had trouble collecting revenue and early on chose to distribute its limited funds to the various private schools around town instead of establishing something more ambitious. Fortunately, the legislature had empowered it to raise funds through a lottery, which made a larger school building possible. In 1830 the board acquired an entire block bounded by Lawrence, Conti, Cedar, and Government streets for less than three thousand dollars and over the next few years managed to pool fifty thousand dollars in lottery funds, a fifteen-thousand-dollar municipal loan, and private donations, including a large one from Hitchcock, for a new school to be named after Representative Barton.[14]

Throughout December 1835, an ad ran in the local paper soliciting bids for a "public schoolhouse . . . the building to be completed by the first of October, 1836."[15] The commissioners' desire was that the edifice be "so constructed as to admit of separate schools for the different ages and sexes embracing different grades of instruction from the infant up to and including the Classics." The three stories were to "conveniently accommodate Six Hundred Scholars."[16] The building committee included Hitchcock and Collins. Dakin was the supervising architect. Once again Thomas James won the contract for the masonry work, while the carpentry, plastering, copper work, ironwork, and landscaping were awarded to others.[17]

Unfortunately for Dakin, the Barton job didn't go nearly as smoothly as the church, and he heard complaints when the October target date wasn't met. On the fifth of that month the building committee reported to the commissioners at large that "sorry to say . . . the building progresses very slowly, and they are fearful that the frost will injure the finishing, or rough casting."[18] This referred to the exterior stucco, which, just as on the church, was to be applied over the brick and scored to simulate ashlar.

The job quickly became more involved than the church, and Dakin had to

Barton Academy's Ionic portico is gently demarcated from busy Government Street by an elegant cast iron fence shipped from New York in 1836.

be extra vigilant certifying work before paying off subcontractors. Problems multiplied. On March 9, 1837, the building committee determined that the mechanics' work needed closer inspection, as the building "is in a condition to be materially injured from the unsound condition in which the roof has been left." The exasperated committee members found that because of the incomplete or improperly finished roof, interior plaster had been exposed to the elements and had fallen to the floor.[19] A month later, the committee examined Dakin's accounts and noted that the figures "appeared correct, but from their complicated character, they have been unable to give them the minute examination which is necessary to report fully."[20]

By the summer of 1837, the building was at last habitable, and the commissioners began meeting upstairs. In September the interior was painted, but it was January 1839 before the finishing touches were finally applied and the shade trees planted around the building.[21] The end product was handsome, to be sure, but Dakin no doubt breathed a sigh of relief when he no longer had to inspect it and deal with the committee's numerous queries and instructions. For their part, the commissioners were saddled with a twelve-thousand-dollar debt, which they partly drew down by renting Barton's rooms to civic groups like the Franklin Society and Masons' Lodge. But there were, at last, children attending class there — in every subject from reading, writing, spelling, and geography to arithmetic. It still wasn't public education, since parents were charged small fees, but it was a significant improvement.[22]

Ever since its completion, Barton Academy's colonnaded rotunda has been visible from as far away as the river, floating above the oak canopy. The building fronts 136 feet on Government Street. Its overall appearance is that of a large, white governmental office building. A heavy first floor supports the slightly smaller second and third stories. The facade is dominated by a pedimented, hexastyle Ionic portico, and the pilastered end pavilions illustrate Gallier and the Dakins' favored wall treatment. The building's most important elements are the dome resting on the Ionic colonnaded rotunda and the surmounting lantern patterned after the Choragic Monument of Lysicrates. Sadly, the interior has been badly chopped up over the decades but originally consisted of a central stair hall with flanking classrooms and offices on all three floors. Today, only the rotunda interior retains any historical integrity. Despite the unsympathetic alterations inside and out, including the loss of the original wooden windows, Barton Academy is listed as a contributing building in the Church Street East Historic District.

As if Charles Dakin didn't have enough to occupy his attentions while the church and Barton were underway, he continued to score major commissions and smaller ones, too. He doesn't appear to have refused any offers. Among these were

(Left) Barton Academy's pillared drum floats above a sea of live oak treetops. This feature's deplorable condition is evident even from a distance. Most of the colonettes atop the lantern have rotted away.

(Right) Mobile's skyline framed by the Ionic columns atop Barton's rapidly deteriorating rotunda. One of the cathedral bell towers is visible just left of center, while the RSA Tower thrusts upward to the right. Centuries of local architectural history are on display from this vantage.

two hotels, a bank, a firehouse, warehouses, brick stores, and private residences, all, alas, since destroyed. Enough documentation exists, however, to demonstrate just how sophisticated and important some of these buildings were.

Not surprisingly, Hitchcock was the motive power behind many of them. Given Mobile's rapid growth and the increasing numbers of people passing through on business and pleasure, he felt it vitally important to the city's wel-

Interior, Barton Academy rotunda. The skill of Mobile's nineteenth-century artisans is apparent in the delicate balustrade and smoothly curved walls. Even the window frames are slightly bowed to compensate for the curvature of the space.

fare that comfortable and commodious lodgings be available. Thus he supplied a lot at the corner of Government and Royal streets, secured the services of the Dakins yet again, and ordered the finest hotel that money could buy. James Dakin probably provided the design, Charles again managed the job, and Collins served as contractor, while the ever-present Thomas James handled the brickwork. Construction started on July 30, 1836, and continued into the fall of 1839. The hotel was by far the most expensive building erected in Mobile up to that time — at more than $200,000 it eclipsed Hobart's courthouse, Beroujon's college building, the hospital, Government Street Presbyterian Church, and even Barton Academy.[23]

The United States Hotel (or Government Street Hotel, as it was sometimes called) strongly resembled Barton Academy from the street, but there were important variations, and its interior appointments were, of course, luxurious compared to the school's spartan furnishings. Rather than an attached portico, the building featured four Corinthian columns in antis on the Royal Street elevation, and its tall vertical windows within the pilastraded walls harkened back more strongly to the Davisean concept than to Barton's smaller rectangular fenestration. Like Barton, a rotunda and metal-roofed dome with a lantern crowned the hotel.

Only slightly less overwhelming was the new Planters and Merchants Bank, which Charles Dakin oversaw through 1837–38. Erected at the northeast corner of Royal and Conti streets, across the street from the hotel, the bank looked like a well-fortified blockhouse with a dome and truncated lantern on top. Hitchcock, practical businessman that he was, no doubt approved of the building's solid form. Among the materials ordered were fifty-seven tons of granite, tens of thousands of bricks, tons of marble for the floors, and mahogany for the countertops. The overall aspect was still Greek Revival, if somewhat clumsily realized, and the local press admired, mostly, the results. "The new and splendid edifice of the Planters & Merchants Bank is just completed," the *Mobile Commercial Register* reported on May 10, 1838, "and is open today for the first time for the transaction of business." The article pronounced the building "a superb one in finish and architectural arrangement. The massive front Portico, and the side view of Conti St. afford as fine and impressive a *tout ensemble* as we have ever seen." Even so, the piece went on to criticize the "awkward and ungainly" dome and regretted that the lantern, though "itself very pretty," was "disproportioned to the cumbersome globe which supports it."

This kind of informed architectural commentary had been unheard of in the local press theretofore and shows just how adroit Mobilians had become at assessing the new buildings around them. To take a walk out Government Street from the river to Broad during the late 1830s amounted to a good alfresco tutorial in the vocabulary of classicism, and no doubt many locals availed themselves of the opportunity. Whatever education they did or didn't have, they must have instinctively known what best pleased the eye. What Hitchcock or the Dakins—especially James, who likely designed the bank—thought of the newspaper's mild criticism is unrecorded.

Not all of the Dakins' commissions involved Hitchcock. These other projects included the St. Michael Street Hotel and the Jonathon Emanuel House, both begun in 1836, Mobile's architectural annus mirabilis. The hotel stood at the northwest corner of St. Michael and Royal streets, mere blocks from the other pillared landmarks springing up downtown, but it was by far the least classical of them all. The building presented a rather plain four-story facade with ranks of rectangular windows and a cornice and low parapet atop. In a clever bit of visual wizardry, the Dakins designed the upper-floor windows a bit shorter than those below, so that from the street they actually appeared to match. The entrance was defined by a pair of Doric pillars in antis, and the street-level bays were delineated by boxy pilasters.

The St. Michael Street Hotel, 1836, the year it was built. From a drawing by James Dakin. (Courtesy Louisiana Division/City Archives, New Orleans Public Library.)

The Emanuel House was constructed at the southwest corner of Government and Joachim streets for the English immigrant and businessman Jonathon Emanuel. Like most of the Port City's elites, Emanuel had numerous real estate holdings and interests, including several brick houses, stores, a stable, and a vacant lot. In 1850 his net worth stood at a staggering $175,000, and his household included a wife and seven children as well as an Irish housekeeper named Catherine O'Brien.[24] At the time his house was built, he was on the board of directors of the Bank of Mobile, the local branch of the Second Bank of the United States (of Nicholas Biddle fame), and the Alabama Life Insurance and Trust Company.[25]

In its form and execution the Emanuel House was one of Mobile's most elegant personal residences — superbly proportioned, perfectly detailed, and handsomely appointed. At three stories high and five bays wide it filled its lot. A one-story portico with fluted Doric columns anchored the smooth facade, and a delicate iron railing above the portico featured such classical symbols as lyres and anthemion crests. The bay immediately over the portico displayed two pairs of engaged slender Ionic columns, and the whole was capped off by a low parapet set off by a projecting cornice. The interior consisted of a central hall with a mahogany staircase, spacious twenty-foot-square high-ceilinged rooms, and silver-plated hardware. A walled garden stood out back.

Such design successes aside, Charles Dakin had to contend with at least one disaster. On November 6, 1836, an entire row of brick stores that he was erecting on Water Street, near the river, collapsed. According to a press account, the as yet unfinished buildings "fell with a tremendous crash. The destruction is complete; hardly one brick remains upon another. The remainder of the row, it is feared, must be taken down."[26] No doubt Dakin was stretched too thin and had become sloppy, and he hadn't used the experienced Thomas James on the job. In his autobiography, Gallier recalled the reversal and inaccurately ascribed Dakin's death to it: "This misfortune so preyed upon the spirits of the poor fellow, that, happening to take a severe cold, a rapid disease of the lungs followed, which carried him off in little more than a year."[27] Gallier's explanation was, in fact, ridiculous, as Charles Dakin quickly cleared away the rubble and, rather than wringing his hands in despair, campaigned for Martin Van Buren for president, bought season tickets for the theater, joined a militia company, and, of course, married in March 1837. In fact, Dakin remained active and effective in both Mobile and New Orleans until his death from yellow fever two years later.[28]

Other builders and architects were active and effective, too, and both formal and vernacular expressions of classical architecture appeared on downtown streets. Hebron Palmer, who had written so enthusiastically about Mobile to Alexander Jackson Davis, most likely designed the Unitarian Church in 1836 (now destroyed), which like Government Street Presbyterian featured a distyle in antis Ionic facade, complete entablature with denticulation, a pedimented front gable, and pilastraded side elevations with full-height windows.[29]

Not far away, Claude Beroujon was laboring on a new cathedral, which Bishop Portier, conscious of holding Catholicism's place amid a surging Protestant population (and their increasingly grand churches), had made a top priority.

The Emanuel House (1836), perhaps the most sophisticated residence ever constructed in Mobile, was torn down shortly after this photograph was taken, in 1936. (Courtesy George B. Rogers Collection, University of South Alabama Archives.)

The cornerstone was laid in 1834, but progress was slow. In 1837 the bishop reported to Rome, "I have spared nothing so that the foundations be solid and durable and in giving to my church a length of 162 foot and a width of 90, I had in mind the future of Mobile and my successors."[30] Like his Protestant colleagues on their projects, Beroujon designed the new cathedral with a distyle in antis facade, but he broke with the Grecian tradition by using elements more appropriate to a Catholic edifice — Roman Doric columns, round-topped windows, and an early basilica plan free of an apse and transepts. The cathedral was not completed until the early 1850s, and subsequent late-nineteenth-century additions significantly changed its appearance (a full portico and flanking towers). During the mid- to late 1830s, however, the cathedral's imposing columns were already contributing to downtown's classical ambience.

In constructing Mobile's earliest residential Greek Revival buildings, architects, contractors, and homeowners were less constrained by rules of order and proportion, and they freely blended classical elements with comfortably familiar Gulf Coast traditions. Even men like James and Beroujon, who were certainly capable of erecting high-style buildings, proved accommodating with less well-heeled or adventurous clients to achieve pleasing results.

Throughout Mobile's colonial and early American periods, the most common house type was the Creole/Gulf Coast cottage. The Creole cottage derives from a long tradition stretching back to the seventeenth-century houses of

Mobile's Cathedral as it appeared ca. 1890. The hexastyle portico added a few years previously, along with the towers here under construction, effectively eclipsed the original distyle in antis configuration. (Courtesy Historic Mobile Preservation Society.)

Normandy — simple side-gabled buildings of one or one and a half stories, usually built of stone. French settlers in the West Indies, the American South, and Canada adapted this basic house type to their climates and locales, in the South often building on brick piers in wood and adding full-length galleries and more steeply pitched gable roofs. Urban examples sometimes lack the front gallery but have an abat-vent, or overhang, along the front eave. A massed floor plan and interior chimneys (which warm the core of the house) are the rule — generally four rooms with back-to-back fireplaces and smaller corner rooms or "cabinets" off the rear porch. In Alabama most of these houses feature two front doors. Louisiana examples with wraparound porches have exterior doors for every room. The lack of interior hallways impressed Benjamin Latrobe, who commented on it in 1819 when he was in New Orleans. Fresh from his northern achievements, Latrobe believed the French thus better employed their interior space.[31]

When the Americans arrived on the Gulf Coast, they found the Creole cottage to be a practical and easy-to-build house, but they preferred a central hall plan, which they had known on the eastern seaboard and in England. Therefore, their usual practice was to keep the basic Creole form but punch through a passage, creating a pair of rooms (or double parlors) to either side. This American or, as it is called locally, Gulf Coast cottage interpretation, otherwise preserved the Creole configuration of a full-length recessed porch under a sweeping side gable roof. Since it would have been inefficient to heat a drafty hallway, however, chimneys were located along outer walls.

The Creole/Gulf Coast cottage was easily embellished with classical elements and details. As the 1830s progressed, local craftsmen played with the form, adding columns, cornices, formal entrances from pattern books like those of Asher Benjamin, pedimented dormers, and interior flourishes like eared architrave door and window surrounds, proving the adaptability and utility of both trends.

Among the most notable extant examples are the Bishop Portier House (1834) and the Hall-Ford House (1836). In each of these, the mix of the vernacular and the formal is so deft, the workmanship so careful, and the result so quintessentially Gulf Coast, that the houses seem almost to have sprung from the earth.

The Bishop Portier House is located at 307 Conti Street, catty-corner from the cathedral. In one of his reports to Rome, Portier described his motivations in building a personal residence. "It was time in 1834 to fix my stay in Mobile," he explained a few years after the fact, "and to give to its Bishop and to its clergy an honorable residence and a handy one, without losing sight, however, of that evangelical simplicity which we preach. The Episcopal house which is composed of ten rooms cost me . . . $7,000."[32]

The reliable Beroujon was given the task of supplying the residence. It is uncertain whether or not he built from scratch or altered an already existing Creole

64 *Chapter Two*

Detail, Portier House main entrance. This highest of classical-style doorways in no way clashes with the house's overall vernacular form. The adaptability of Greek Revival elements and details assured their success in the Port City.

The Portier House (1834) successfully employs a number of classical features. Its walled garden was once typical of downtown residences. Sadly, only a few remain.

cottage. Whatever the case, his achievement was to tastefully merge old and new. The overall form and some details are well within the Creole/Gulf Coast cottage vein — a high foundation, frame construction, casement first-story windows, a gable roof parallel to the street, and a central hall. But his stylistic touches distinguish the whole and admirably fulfill Portier's mandate that it be at once honorable, handy, and simple. They include Tuscan porch columns; a smooth, plastered facade; a door framed by pilasters topped by a full entablature with, amazingly, a frieze containing triglyphs and metopes; and three segmental arched dormers with denticulation and sash flanked by unfluted colonettes. Portier must have watched with great satisfaction from his own columned gallery as the cathedral slowly rose to eye level and then beyond.

The Hall-Ford House stands at 165 St. Emanuel Street. Edward Hall, a native Philadelphian who arrived in Mobile during the early 1820s and established himself as a successful commission merchant, bought the lot in 1834 and began construction shortly thereafter. Unfortunately, as is typical with many early houses, the builder is unknown, but he was obviously grounded in folkways as well as the new Greek Revival style.[33]

The two-and-a-half-story house occupies most of its 66-foot by 116-foot lot. The first story is brick covered in stucco scored to simulate ashlar, while the upper stories are frame (except the second-story facade, which is stucco over

The Hall-Ford House, ca. 1900. The dropped awnings over the first- and second-story entrances provided much needed relief from the westering sun. The windows could be shuttered. (Courtesy Mobile Historic Development Commission.)

Column detail, Hall-Ford House. During a recent restoration project, the crumbling porch columns were braced by modern timbers so that masons could tuck-point the brick and restucco the exterior.

lath). Kick-off shed roofs (attached rather than under the main roofline of the house and slightly angled) shelter the front and rear porches, and three dormers punctuate the roof. The first-story porch is supported by well-proportioned brick and plaster Doric columns, and the second-story porch by wooden ones. Fluted pilasters define each end of the first-story facade, the doorway features sidelights and a transom, and the second story includes jibbed windows with full-height shutters. The interior plan consists of central hallways on each floor with flanking rooms. Original hardware, including Carpenter locks, and wood graining on the wide parlor doors, is present. The rear courtyard, sheltered by the main house, a rear ell, and a two-story brick servants' wing, is a rare survivor of once-common downtown amenities.

Not all houses built during these years were so strongly vernacular, however. Just as Oakleigh is a more formal Greek Revival expression, other residences reflected a thorough application of classical principles. These included a consecutive trio of two-story columned edifices on Church Street, one purported to have belonged to Hitchcock, and the Ottenstein House at 207–9 North Jackson Street (all destroyed). The latter was a two-story duplex Thomas James erected

Ottenstein House (1836). Thomas S. James built this double house for rental purposes. It was torn down in 1940, shortly after this photograph was taken. (Courtesy Library of Congress.)

in 1836. With its heavy, two-story porch and beetling entablature, it fit well within the Greek mode.

The Beal-Hunter House at 205 North Conception Street is altogether one of the most pleasing Greek Revival residences to survive from the period. Built in 1836 by Gustavus Beal, himself a builder, developer, and likely his own architect, this modest yet graceful structure nicely adapts a Grecian vocabulary to a cottage scale and plan. Like Oakleigh, the Beal-Hunter House displays a temple front, and its facade consists of flush wooden siding as is so typical on Greek Revival residences. Six Doric columns fashioned in cypress support the porch, and a quartet of wide doorways demonstrates the importance of climate in local architecture. The interior plan consists of four massed rooms and two central

The Beal-Hunter House (1836) displays a graceful one-story temple front that is both pleasing and restful to the eye.

chimneys, but this Creole arrangement is utterly overwhelmed from the street by the strong Doric facade.

As 1836 rolled into 1837, local merchants, builders, and boosters must have felt as though they were living a dream. On seemingly every block construction was underway, and brickyards, sawmills, sash and door outfits, and hardware and furniture stores were enjoying good business. Every able-bodied man who wanted to could find well-paying, meaningful work, and ships and steamboats filled the river. Money flowed like water, and men got rich by their wits alone. In just a few short years, downtown Mobile had been transformed into a wonderland of classical porticoes, columns, rotundas, and cornices. Hitchcock spoke the truth when he declared, "Our city may be said to have been built during the ten year period before 1837."[34] But a reckoning was just around the corner, and the dream was about to become a nightmare.

In March 1836, President Andrew Jackson at last triumphed over Nicholas Biddle in the long-running "bank war" and succeeded in denying the recharter of the Second Bank of the United States. State and local banks now received all government deposits and, in turn, offered loans at steep discounts, which encouraged wild speculation in real estate and imports. It was all fueled by paper money, however, and when the government required payments in hard currency, the banks reneged on their discounts, and the economy was thrown into a full-fledged depression. In his comical 1853 account *The Flush Times of Alabama and Mississippi*, Joseph G. Baldwin recalled the consequences. "Men worth a million were insolvent for two millions," he wrote; "promising young cities marched back again into wilderness. The ambitious town plat was reannexed to the plantation, like a country girl taken home from the city. The frolic was ended, and what headaches, and feverish limbs the next morning!"[35]

In Mobile the panic's effects became steadily more enervating over the course of 1837. Everybody suffered. Out at Oakleigh, James Roper, wealthy on paper but cash poor, suddenly found himself insolvent. In an effort to compensate, he began selling off slaves, whose value was rapidly declining along with that of everything else in town. But he was luckier than most when his brother-in-law intervened, bought the remaining slaves and Oakleigh, and allowed Roper and his family to continue residing on the property.[36]

Real estate values plummeted. Between 1831 and 1837, the city's real property had skyrocketed from just over a million dollars to more than twenty-seven million. But the following years were telling — value declined to twenty million dollars in 1838 and further to thirteen million in 1840. Local banks, including the brand new Planters and Merchants, folded, and city fathers watched helplessly as tax revenues dried up and the mounting municipal debt threatened ruin.[37]

Like a deflated balloon, Mobile's economy collapsed. On May 6, 1837, a business publication reported on the bleak scene: "Business is in the same flat condition that it has been for weeks past. Everything is dull enough in the way of trade. The lawyers and Sheriff are the only busy men in town. Money continues to withdraw from the merchants and traders and all other men's hands, except those in the banks, and a few misers besides."[38] Before the month was out, the city was officially bankrupt.

Construction was severely curtailed or entirely stopped. In July, Charles Dakin and Collins were forced to reassess their plans for the United States Hotel and decided to leave off the fifth story.[39] Within months the stagnation was so bad that the young architect closed the branch office and rejoined his brother in the Crescent City.[40] Portier's projects weren't faring any better. In

March 1838, as he contemplated the stalled work on his cherished cathedral, not to mention the personal suffering around him, he wrote to a fellow bishop up north, "We have become here hardened in misery, with no hope of sudden change."[41]

But Hitchcock was the biggest loser and, by extension, hundreds of families and the city itself. By April 1837, his circumstances were dire. He engaged in frequent correspondence with Nicholas Biddle, whose bank held his notes, and he traveled north in an attempt to rearrange his affairs and remain solvent. He failed. In a letter to the Reverend Hamilton, he displayed a calm detachment about his bankruptcy and even looked forward to a removal "from the entanglements of business." He continued, "Though I cannot serve my friends with my purse, I will endeavour to do what is better, by exhibiting an example of what can be done without it."[42]

As Hitchcock made his way south by steamboat, his family and community remained true. In a heartfelt letter, his wife reassured him of her devotion and admiration. She wrote that she would be "happy and honored to share your poverty and your sorrows." She further informed him that his friends and neighbors were prepared to offer "every consolation" and closed with a wish that he hurry home "to the arms of her, who is more devotedly than ever your wife."[43]

When at last he arrived, Hitchcock encountered an outpouring of support. On May 6 a committee of Mobile tradesmen, including Collins and Thomas James, lauded him as "the firm friend and warm patron of the mechanical interests" and invited him to a public dinner in his honor.[44] Deeply humbled, Hitchcock demurred but expressed his confidence that the hard times would pass and that he would once again "prosecute those improvements, both useful and ornamental, which are now only commenced; but which are destined to make our city the pride of the state and the resort of the intelligent, enterprising and virtuous."[45]

It wasn't in Hitchcock's nature to remain idle for long, and in the winter of 1838 he finagled a deal with his largest creditor for a $100,000 loan that would allow him to improve his vacant properties, generate income, and thereby pay down his debt. He secured the loan (at a punishing 18 to 24 percent) by mortgaging some of his properties for embarrassingly low figures compared to their original worth. Temporarily flush, Hitchcock embarked on a frenzied construction schedule, erecting brick stores, a livery stable capable of holding one hundred horses, warehouses, and a "mammoth press" for the cotton trade. In a letter to his brother, Hitchcock estimated that all told he had laid two million bricks, employed six hundred men, "and support three or four times that number." His payroll was an astonishing $10,000 a week.[46]

But Hitchcock's plans were dashed only months later when the bank ignored the verbal arrangement he had foolishly depended upon with them and called in its loan. Not yet far enough along in his development scheme to create serious income, Hitchcock couldn't pay. Frantically, he attempted to convince the bank to reconsider and personally appealed to Biddle, but to no avail. The situation remained a legal and financial tangle far beyond Hitchcock's untimely death in the summer of 1839.[47]

Amid the disruption the *Mobile Commercial Register* surveyed the scene and, incredibly, found a ray of hope. On May 10, 1838, the paper confidently remarked "suspension is now about the only relic of the misfortunes of last year. When that ceases, the elastic energies of the country will reassert their power, and the reed which has been, not prostrated by the storm, will again stand firm and erect in its natural strength and grace."[48] Though some no doubt scoffed, there was at least a little activity left in the building trades, evidenced by the arrival of bricks and scaffolding at the site of a proposed new Episcopal church near the river. The resulting building would be one of the city's finest.

Mobile's first Episcopalians worshipped with their Protestant neighbors in a frame union church at Church and St. Emanuel streets throughout the 1820s. But just as the Presbyterians grew and established their own presence on Government Street, the Episcopalians formally organized themselves on February 26, 1828, and named their unimposing little building Christ Church. The structure was in poor condition, and in December 1834 the floor collapsed beneath the weight of the faithful. When one considers that most frame buildings were a good two to three feet off the ground on brick piers, such an event was not only embarrassing but dangerous. Services were temporarily moved elsewhere, while efforts were made to erect a more suitable structure on the site.[49]

The building committee included several men with superior architectural bona fides — Edward Hall, William Alderson, and Jonathon Emanuel — and not surprisingly proved more than equal to the task. On November 30, 1835, two designs were reviewed from "many" received. These included a Gothic-style structure, estimated to cost $45,000, and a "Grecian Doric Building 70 feet front and 96 feet deep with a bell tower of 109 feet from the doorstep, calculated to contain 114 pews on the ground floor." The latter design's estimated cost was $38,000, so the committee recommended it.[50]

Because Christ Church is so obviously a New York building in the Town and Davis tradition — distyle in antis portico, pilastraded sides, and Davisean windows — some have speculated that Gallier or the Dakins were somehow responsible for its design. The cornerstone was laid in 1835 and the contract inked August 6, 1838, but there is no mention of either Gallier or the Dakins in it or any other extant records. The contract lists Cary W. Butt as architect and James Barnes as the contractor.[51] On April 20, 1840, a report of the Building Committee lists payments of $150 to Butt and $160 to Frederick Bunnell "for plans."[52]

A somewhat fanciful view of Christ Episcopal Church in 1840. In actuality, the exterior brick was not covered by stucco until twelve years later. The hurricane of 1906 toppled the steeple, which the current congregation plans to restore. (Courtesy of the Museum of Mobile.)

Facade detail, Christ Episcopal Church. The triglyphs and metopes were added after the 1906 storm. This building's strong Doric lines are softened for pedestrians by sinuous live oak tree limbs in the foreground.

Butt, of course, had done a little drafting for the Dakins before hanging out his own shingle in 1837, and Bunnell was soon to design the U.S. Marine Hospital, adjacent to the City Hospital on St. Anthony Street. Both men obviously were attuned to the New York architects' importance, ability, and influence and no doubt saw imitation as the surest route to fame and fortune. That Butt was no mean architect is further evidenced by his design of the Florida state house in 1839. Barring further documentary evidence, the design for Christ Church should therefore be credited to Butt, with Bunnell likely providing assistance with construction drawings. But the building's intellectual pedigree must be routed through Gallier and the Dakins to the Town and Davis wellspring.

The contract was meticulous and laid out everything wanted, along with the requisite dimensions and finishes. The building committee required that the stonework (door and window sills, steps, portico pavers) "be of the same kind and quality as that used in the New Bank on Royal Street," a reference to the Planters and Merchants and a clear indication that the Dakins' buildings were now Mobile's architectural gold standard. The contract further mandated that

Christ Episcopal Church has held its corner with quiet dignity for more than 150 years. Live oaks shade its facade, while Mobile Government Plaza looms in the background.

the fourteen windows consist of forty-eight panes each (the stained glass came much later), which would admit plenty of light, and the ceiling was to be elliptical with a plain cornice.[53] The spectacular steeple with its thorough Greek detailing was far more sophisticated than the somewhat clunky tower perched atop Government Street Presbyterian Church.

The job went fairly well — Butt and Barnes were fortunately spared the headaches that plagued Charles Dakin over at Barton Academy. Even so, the planned stucco exterior finish would not be supplied until 1852. In the meantime, the sanctuary pleased everyone and represented an important step for the Episcopalians. On January 25, 1840, the newspaper announced that the church was almost ready for services, and shortly thereafter Bishop Leonidas Polk of the Louisiana and Alabama Diocese consecrated the building.[54]

As the 1830s drew to a close, Mobilians doubtless took pride in what had been accomplished. A new map produced by an itinerant cartographer named John La Tourette handsomely showcased their greatest civic and architectural achievements — Barton Academy, the United States Hotel, City Hospital, and Government Street Presbyterian Church — and the map's Greek key border seemed only appropriate for their pillared city. Despite the lingering economic malaise, the future held promise. The city's population was approaching twelve thousand, and cotton prices were sure to rise, starting everything up again.[55]

The 1838 La Tourette map celebrated Greek Revival Mobile. (Courtesy Library of Congress.)

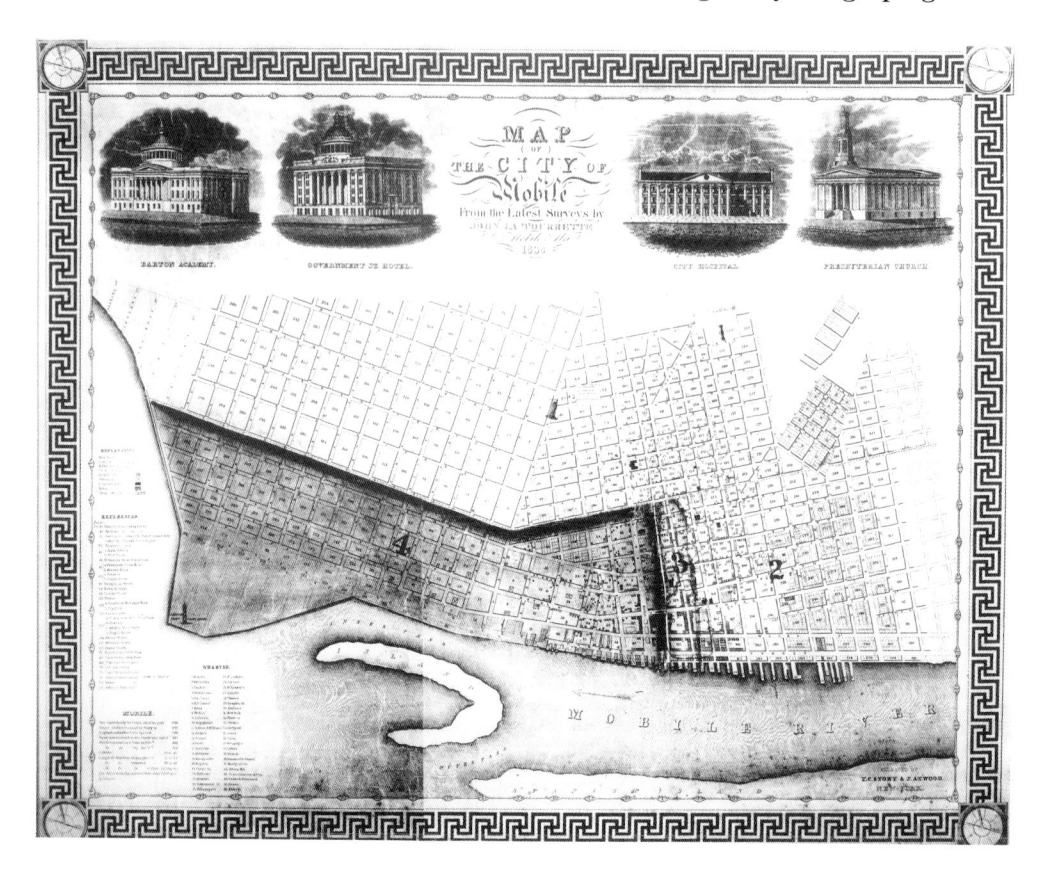

On January 2, 1839, the *Mobile Commercial Register* reported a happy and safe holiday season. Among the recent activities had been an orphans benefit fair, "a perfect jam of happy, benevolent faces," and a boat race on the river, "the wharves and vessels and their rigging . . . crowded with spectators." Of New Year's Eve, the paper noted, "The evening was pleasantly passed in social assemblages . . . closing a beautiful day with a lovely night, harbingers we hope of a bright future."

On February 15, city fathers made arrangements for a Washington's Birthday parade, to include the First Volunteer Regiment.[56] But not everyone in town was happy, as quickly became apparent when a carpenters' riot rocked the peace. What with the economic downturn, paying work was harder to come by, and the continuing influx of outsiders riled the resident tradesmen. Convinced that these newcomers were driving down wages, a band of local mechanics attacked a shop where immigrants were known to live and work. According to a press account, "The windows and doors were driven in, some furniture destroyed, and the proprietor of the premises, the contractor, and the workmen, narrowly escaped lynching." A hastily dispatched fire company arrested "the spirit of misrule," but local authorities were rattled by the incident.[57]

In March, the English parliamentarian and world traveler J. S. Buckingham arrived in Mobile to present a lecture series at the Presbyterian Church. Unaware of any social unrest, his first impressions of the city were favorable. He found the streets along the waterfront "spacious and commodious," and he thought Government Street, "lined with rows of trees on either hand, protected by an excellent flag-pavement at the sides, and already ornamented with some exceedingly handsome public structures, and private mansions and dwellings," about the prettiest thoroughfare he had yet seen. "Of the public buildings," he wrote, "the most prominent and the most beautiful is Barton Academy." Nearly as impressive was the Presbyterian church, "the largest and most beautiful" religious edifice in town. Oddly, Buckingham didn't like the exterior so much, which he dismissed as "not in the best taste," but he was suitably awed by the "strikingly beautiful" interior, "unsurpassed," he declared, "in chasteness of style and elegance of decoration in the United States." He especially liked the "happy union of the Egyptian and Greek, in the elevated platform . . . and the semi-Theban and semi-Corinthian portico, which seems to rise behind the platform, with the rich diagonally-indented ceiling." Also noteworthy were the "luxurious sofa-like pews." Closer to the river, he was surprised by the size and quality of the United States Hotel, "which when finished, will be much larger, and certainly much handsomer than either the Astor House at New York, the Tremont House at Boston, or the American Hotel at Buffalo, the three largest and handsomest at present in the Union."[58]

Once he had the opportunity to observe the city a little more closely, Buckingham discovered less seemly places, foremost among them the grogshops, filled with "numbers of well-dressed young men . . . smoking cigars, and drinking wine, spirits, and cordials, at an early hour of the day." Buckingham believed Mobilians' propensity to drink explained the high crime rate, frequent duels, and numerous small fires.[59]

Late spring and summer brought oppressive heat and humidity, continued commercial torpor, and the gnawing fear of scourges like yellow fever and cholera. Those who could escaped to safer climes up north, out to Spring Hill, or over to the elevated bluffs of Mobile Bay's Eastern Shore. For the rest, the days passed uneventfully until early August, when the dreaded yellow fever arrived with a vengeance. It would turn out to be one of the worst visitations in the city's history, with a death toll above six hundred souls. Many years later, Rev. Hamilton recalled the epidemic in a sermon for a new congregation in Warren, Pennsylvania. "For weeks, for months in succession," Hamilton told his rapt listeners, "my sole employment was to pass from one sick bed to another — from one grave to another — from one house of bereavement to another — to save life if possible or to soothe the suffering and to comfort the sorrowing."[60]

One of the earliest victims was Hitchcock, who fell ill on August 5, the very day he was elected to the state legislature. The Reverend Hamilton attended him as closely as was possible, given the general emergency, and in a subsequent funeral discourse, recalled the judge's final moments. Hamilton sadly noted that despite a "vigorous constitution," Hitchcock steadily worsened, and "his look and manner showed that he himself was more fully aware of his danger, than were his family, who very naturally clung to the last ray of hope." When the pastor asked if his worldly affairs were in order, Hitchcock said that they were and announced, "I am ready to die." He admitted that it was "hard to part with my family," but he had no fears as to his salvation. His wife was not so calm and wailed, "Oh! my husband, my counsellor, my friend; when you are gone, I shall be alone — no friend! — what shall I do? — oh! what shall I do?" His breathing labored, Hitchcock clutched his wife, pulled her to him, and hoarsely whispered, "Trust in God! Trust in God! Trust in God!" He then beckoned to Hamilton and begged him to deliver a message to the congregation that had been his refuge amid so many recent travails. "Tell them to love one another truly and tenderly," he said. After bidding his children and servants good-bye, Hitchcock ceased his struggles "about twenty minutes past 6 o'clock, on the morning of Sunday August 11th."[61]

Reaction was immediate and widespread. The *Mobile Commercial Register* wrote, "The sudden demise of this distinguished citizen has sent a thrill through every part of this community." In a long obituary, the paper singled out Hitchcock's construction efforts as especially noteworthy: "For many years he has been a judicious friend to the industrious mechanic, employing his extensive means in improving the city, adorning it with buildings for the several purposes of business, of public education, and charity, and thus furnishing constant employment and certain support to a large number of industrious men and their families. Almost every street of our city bears the impress of his enterprise, his liberality, or his taste."[62]

Within days, a citizens committee was formed (Collins was a member) and drafted a series of resolutions relating to Hitchcock. "Our feelings and sympathies cluster around his bereaved and afflicted family," the committee declared. "With them we mourn their loss with them we must bow submissively to the stroke. Our tears with theirs commingle at his honored grave, and a grateful city with one voice mourns a benefactor." Committee members voted to formally extend their sympathies to the family and, with its consent, determined to "erect a marble monument to his memory." In a touching gesture, the committee concluded that every citizen would have the right to contribute to the monument fund.[63]

Thus ended the life of a most remarkable man. In his impact on his adopted city, Henry Hitchcock was a veritable Nicholas Biddle. During the few years

The Three Sisters were built in 1835–36 at the southwest corner of Church and Jackson streets under Henry Hitchcock's auspices. Oral tradition held that Hitchcock himself lived in one of them, but city directories do not confirm this. Nonetheless, the homes are further evidence of his remarkable impact on his adopted city. All three were demolished in 1964. (From Artwork of Mobile and Vicinity, *Chicago: W. H. Parish Publishing, 1894.)*

that he was able to enjoy health and prosperity, Hitchcock established himself as a model of integrity and public spirit and, in the process, taught his fellow citizens not only how to behave, but how to build for the ages.[64]

A month beyond Hitchcock's death, the epidemic continued unabated all along the Gulf Coast. On September 12, the *New Orleans Daily Picayune* surveyed Mobile's situation and reported, "The clouds of sickness which now hang over our sister city look even more lowering and gloomy than those which darken our own." Not surprisingly, business remained sluggish. "The banks are open but two hours a day," the article continued. "The offices and stores are nearly all closed, and the business haunts present a most gloomy and desolate appearance." Unfortunately, worse was to come.

Since the 1827 fire, Mobile's authorities and citizens had taken numerous practical steps to lessen the risk of another such misfortune. At least eight volunteer fire companies were formed, water reservoirs and a wooden pipe and cast iron hydrant system were put in place, frame construction was disallowed downtown, brick firewalls were required for row buildings, and a property guard created. The latter group's task was to move ahead of the flames and rescue furniture, valuables, and personal possessions; place them in a pile; and protect them from "all idle and disorderly persons."[65]

Despite these precautions, a series of early October fires devastated the city. The conditions were eerily similar to those of 1827—an ongoing drought, a reduced population, and gusty winds. At the time, arson was strongly suspected, and years later at least two different men would indeed claim the credit.

The first fire started on Wednesday, October 2. Given what was to follow, it was relatively minor. About 10:30 that evening a Dauphin Street furniture store erupted in flames, which quickly spread up and down the block, consuming a number of buildings. The damage, though considerable, was not especially notable in an era when such blazes were common occurrences in all American cities. Not so the conflagration of October 7, which started early evening in a nondescript wooden shed at Dauphin and Conception streets and rapidly roared through the neighboring frame outbuildings and tenements. In a desperate bid to create firebreaks, police and militia rousted out panicked inhabitants (some of them feverish and bedridden) and blew up their residences with kegs of black powder. The next day, a commission merchant named Duke Goodman wrote to a friend that his own house had been among those blasted to smithereens. All was not lost, however. "I saved pretty much all my furniture," he was relieved to report. Unfortunately, many others were not so lucky.[66]

By the time this fire was brought under control, the scope and cost of the destruction were staggering. Much of Dauphin Street between Conception and Franklin streets was in ashes, as were several blocks along either side. In all, five hundred buildings were burned, hundreds of people were made homeless, and the property loss was estimated at well over a million dollars. To add outrage to the tragedy, according to a newspaper account, "the origin of the fire is attributed to incendiaries; and we understand that two persons were seized on suspicion and lodged in jail. Can it be possible there can be found in human shape, such base, fiendish monsters? Mobile seems indeed a doomed city. Have we not drank deep enough of the bitter cup of adversity and affliction? When will our calamities end?"[67]

The answer was "not yet," for in the wee hours of October 9, still another conflagration purged the downtown. This one began in an unoccupied room at the Mansion House Hotel at the southeast corner of Conti and Royal streets, soon engulfed the building, and then threatened the nearby Planters and Merchants Bank and the almost-completed United States Hotel. The city's exhausted firemen, grimy and distracted by their personal losses, nonetheless heroically battled the fire "to the last cistern." Not far away on Government Street, the Reverend Hamilton's nineteen-year-old son Thomas struggled from his sickbed, determined to join his company, the Phoenix No. 6, as it fought the flames. Young Hamilton was so weakened that he couldn't walk, however, and instead dragged himself down the block, helplessly watching the holocaust. Those who were able to contest the fire were quickly overwhelmed as flames leaped far into the sky and embers showered the surrounding blocks. The roar was audible from three miles away.[68]

The October 9, 1839, fire. The Mansion House Hotel burns in the background, while the United States Hotel (right) and the Planters and Merchants Bank (left) are as yet untouched. Note the personal belongings piled up in the foreground on Royal Street. (Courtesy Historic Mobile Preservation Society.)

The bank and hotel were soon enveloped. The heat was so intense that the bank's dome spontaneously burst into flame. Firemen had no hope of climbing that high fast enough, and even if they could have, water supplies and pressures were woefully unequal to the task. Horrified Mobilians could only watch as fire shot out the windows of their architectural crown jewels, reducing them to gutted shells.[69]

Numerous northern papers reported the disastrous succession of fires. In a detailed account, the *Pennsylvanian* put the loss after the October 7 blaze at better than half a million dollars. "Upwards of twenty houses were blown up," the paper relayed, "and about one thousand persons rendered homeless, and almost every article of their property destroyed."[70] The *Philadelphia Courier* stated simply, "All is confusion, excitement and distress."[71] Locally, the *Mobile Commercial Register*, like its readers, was stricken. "Mobile looks more like a beleaguered town, battered by the cannon of a foreign enemy, and hourly looking for a final assault from some unknown quarter, than a commercial city in a time of peace and abundance," the paper sadly reported. "We walk among ruins, some of which threaten to topple down upon our heads."[72] The only consolation was that Hitchcock hadn't been there to see it.

Though numerous vagrants and other suspicious characters were arrested, the blame was never satisfactorily placed. Who could have done such a thing? Several years later, an escaped slave said that he had been partly responsible. According to an account printed in a local paper, the man explained that he had been in Mobile that summer and, along with about one hundred other slaves, held secret meetings outside of town about how best to free themselves. Their first plan was to murder the whites, but they worried about ferocious reprisals. They then set upon the plan "to burn the city" as a distraction, allowing them to flee amid the confusion.[73] Fortunately for Mobile's already oppressed black population, authorities had no intimation of this at the time.

In 1857 yet another man claimed to have been involved, and in subsequent years his account was given some credence. In a long confession to a Mississippi sheriff, the notorious outlaw James Copeland said that his gang started the fires as a diversion after they had looted several Dauphin Street stores. According to Copeland, some of his men had infiltrated the city guards, and on a night when they had the first watch, the burglars slipped into town disguised "with false whiskers, some with a green patch over one eye, and many of them dressed like sailors." Armed with knives and revolvers, they systematically broke into the deserted stores, robbing them and setting fires as they left. Back lit by a lurid red glow, the men hauled their plunder down to the river, where they slipped away with it aboard small skiffs. Copeland claimed their total take was worth more than $25,000 and included silver, fine silks, muslins, gold watches, and clothing.[74] Given that Dauphin Street in particular was so heavily damaged by the October 2 and 7 fires, Copeland's story appears plausible.

With November's frosts, the yellow fever at last released its grip upon the city, and those who had fled returned. They were appalled by what they found. "We have dismal sights to show them in a blackened district," the *Merchants and Planters Journal* glumly wrote. "We can lead them to the ruins of some of the finest public buildings and point them to smoldering heaps of what were once our most frequented and popular hotels." But that wasn't the worst of it. "A still more melancholy duty will fall to us who have lived through the perils and terrors of the times to count up the losses, greater than those of the houses and hotels . . . that fill a thousand hearts with a sense of profound loneliness and deep, if not bitter, regret, to call over the roll of the dead."[75]

There was some cause for optimism, however. Many buildings still stood — including the warehouses, cotton presses, and offices along the river as well as numerous churches and public buildings — and upstate cotton needed a viable port if it was to find its way out to the world. The editor at the *Merchants and Planters Journal* consoled himself with such thoughts and concluded, "We shall show how much of the spirit of the time there is left among us, and what a flourishing city we can make of this Mobile of ours."[76]

CHAPTER THREE

TOWN AND COUNTRY

CLASSICISM,

1840–1865

In the decades that followed the disastrous 1830s, Mobile slowly recovered its balance and by the eve of the Civil War was once again a prosperous place. The spectacular growth and landmark architectural achievements of the late 1830s gave way to a sedate period of modest construction in a variety of styles. The Greek Revival was no longer dominant, but it remained influential and important. The city's elites moved out to surrounding areas like Spring Hill and the Eastern Shore, and erected comfortable country retreats that were easy blends of the Greek Revival and the vernacular. Closer in, architects and builders adapted a classical vocabulary to urban forms like firehouses, town houses, and row houses. They also experimented with the Italianate (adding ornate cast iron verandahs) and Gothic Revival styles for residences, public buildings, and churches. In the mid-1850s, ever alert to shifting tastes, these builders creatively paired the Italianate and Greek Revival with handsome results.

The brickyards, sawmills, lumberyards, and various stores that served the building trades recovered along with the economy, and the local cadre of tradesmen grew in numbers and skill. During the Civil War, Mobile was justifiably famous for its coastal ambience and architectural flair. But before it could become the "Paris of the Confederacy," its citizens first had to deal with 1839's emotional aftermath.[1]

"Stand from under!" blared a small notice in the February 15, 1840, edition of the *Mobile Commercial Register*. "The walls of the Merchants and Planters Bank are about to be pulled down. We are requested by the Architect to warn all sidewalkers to stand from under." Just who the "Architect" was is a mystery, but it certainly wasn't Charles Dakin, who had abandoned Mobile for New Orleans during the worst of the panic and shortly thereafter succumbed to yellow fever. It could well have been his brother, because the new bank that was eventually erected strongly resembled the original, but no records survive to confirm this.

If James Dakin did design the new bank, it marked the end of his remarkably productive involvement with Mobile's built environment.[2]

The months immediately after the 1839 fires were filled with the unpleasant tasks of burying the last of the fever victims, demolishing dangerous ruins, and clearing away literally tons of charred timbers, baked bricks, broken slate, and the even sadder detritus of domestic life — smashed furniture, sopping carpet, chipped crockery, partially melted silverware, burned shoes, and ruined toys.

Less than a month after the last fire, the drought broke, and drenching rains turned acres of black and gray ash into a sticky, smelly paste, driving almost everyone indoors. A writer for the *New Orleans Daily Picayune* was undeterred, however, and toured the town. "All was now desolate, but presenting a certain grandeur, even in ruins," he observed. At the site of the United States Hotel, he paused to study "the walls and lofty arches of the interior." His reverie was rudely interrupted when the massive Corinthian columns fronting Royal Street suddenly crashed down. "They fell nearly perpendicularly," he wrote, "and the roaring sound which they made startled the whole neighborhood and the shock made the solid earth shake sensible to a considerable distance." The rubble completely blocked the street.[3]

Because the city was broke, municipal authorities were ill equipped to embark on a reconstruction program. The *London Morning Post* chided from abroad, "It must be considered a great reproach to the inhabitants to allow so wealthy and flourishing a place to be less circumspect, in this particular, than the various other cities of the Union, which have likewise contracted loans for the purpose of effecting local improvements."[4] Whatever shame officials might have felt had, of course, been eclipsed by the more recent disasters of pestilence and fire. City fathers were also worried about free blacks and slaves taking advantage of official distraction to congregate around grogshops and disturb the peace or plot insurrection.[5]

During the early 1840s, travelers found Mobile to be a generally busy port but were repulsed by its lack of order and cleanliness. In early May 1840, the Reverend William H. Wills arrived in town after a long and disagreeably hot steamboat trip down the Tombigbee River. He had to dodge cotton bales everywhere — on the boat, the dock, and even on the sidewalks near the river. In his diary Wills conceded that Mobile might be a pleasant place to live in the summer, "but little attention is paid it by the authorities. Hence it is dirty and about the wharves very filthy and stinking." He noted the recent fire damage, "the fairest and best portions of the city in ashes," and the fact that troublesome small blazes were still common —"only ten days ago they had a fire and 3000 bales of cotton were destroyed."[6]

Four years later, conditions weren't any better, as the German amateur paleontologist Albert C. Koch revealed in his travel account. "I was astonished by the filthiness of the city of Mobile," he recalled. "When we left the steamboat an atmosphere of horrible odors met us, permeating all the dirty streets which were bordered on both sides with green gutters."[7]

Henry Whipple, the Minnesota bishop who so admired Philadelphia's Girard College, spent enough time in Mobile to get beyond first impressions, and his account provides a more rounded picture than those of Koch or Wills. "There are but few fine buildings in the city and it appears to be a place of business rather than of pleasure," Whipple wrote, echoing pre-1835 travelers' descriptions of the Port City. Nonetheless, he found places that he liked. "Some of the back streets are beautiful, and out of the city in the piny woods are some beautiful residences of the aristocracy." Like almost everyone else, however, he thought the streets a trial, "worse than any I have ever seen. The transition from wet to dry is so sudden that one is either wading in mud or suffocating with dust."[8]

Whipple was intrigued by Mobile's rich human mosaic and penned a colorful description of some of its character types. "Here is a sailor just on shore with a pocket full of rocks ready for devilment of any kind and there is a beggar in rags. Pretty Creoles, pale faced sewing girls, painted vice, big headed and little headed men, tall anatomies & short Falstaffs, all are seen each full of himself & as if isolated from the world, so full do all seem of themselves. Oh! what an array of knowledge boxes, what a diversity of bread baskets, a great country this and no mistake."[9]

One of the "knowledge boxes" that Whipple had the occasion to study more closely was the Reverend Hamilton, whom he heard give a sermon at the Presbyterian church. "Mr. H. is a powerful preacher," Whipple wrote, "altho he has an affected way with him which detracts from his eloquence. I believe his peculiar manners are natural to him, yet to me they are unpleasant."[10] Whipple elaborated no further on these mannerisms, and since no one else who knew Hamilton seems to have mentioned them, they must remain a mystery.

Whipple commented on virtually everything in town — the rough manners and hearty fare in the hotels, a slave auction, the public markets with their profusion of fruits and vegetables, and even a visit by Henry Clay. Notably absent, however, is any detailed architectural commentary. He mentioned Hamilton's church, but only in passing, and paid no heed to Barton Academy or Christ Church. What most impressed the Minnesota bishop was the city's frontier aspect and stimulating range of personalities.[11] This was perhaps to be expected, given that so much had simply been swept away.

Compared to the prior incredible building boom, construction during the 1840s was an anemic enterprise. City officials couldn't do much but did manage to erect a pesthouse, a new jail, and an armory. Bishop Portier pushed doggedly

U.S. Marine Hospital. (From Artwork of Mobile and Vicinity, *Chicago: W. H. Parish Publishing, 1894.)*

on at the cathedral, and Christ Church was almost finished at St. Emanuel Street. The decade's most important new Greek Revival buildings were the U.S. Marine Hospital and a few urban and country residences.[12]

The Marine Hospital was a federally funded endeavor, and local architects and builders scrambled for such a plum commission. Congress established the Marine Hospital Service in 1798 to care for sick and disabled sailors. Mobile had a frame Marine Hospital on Government Street at the head of Marine Street, but it burned in 1836, and a plan to replace it ground slowly into gear. A large plot of land was purchased adjacent to the new City Hospital in 1838, and the following April, architectural drawings and contractors' bids were solicited by J. B. Hogan, the local customs collector.[13]

Hogan arranged for John K. Collins to review the proposals as they came in. Collins, of course, had managed the recent City Hospital job. James Barnes, a carpenter and contractor who was at work on Christ Church and apparently anxious to upgrade his status to architect and contractor, submitted a strong entry. Barnes was on the verge of being chosen when Frederick Bunnell, who had a little drafting on the Christ Church job under his belt as well as a more formal stock of architectural knowledge, submitted an alternate set of drawings. Hogan noted that Bunnell's set "came nearer our wants than the first" and was cheaper besides. Bunnell got the nod, and Robert Williamson, a bricklayer, won the contractor's portion of the $17,500 commission. Construction began and must have seemed a godsend for the area's job-hungry tradesmen. The first patients were admitted in 1843.[14]

Today the former U.S. Marine Hospital houses the Mobile County Health

Department. It and the old City Hospital, taken together, present an impressive monumental Greek Revival tableau. At 161 feet by 62 feet, the Marine Hospital is almost the same dimensions as the City Hospital and is also brick covered in stucco. Its original interior plan was, like that of the City Hospital, a central hall with a bisecting cross-hall running the length of the building. Despite the similarities, however, there are important differences between the buildings. The Marine Hospital's facade employs a classical vocabulary in altogether different fashion. Rather than three stories like the City Hospital, the Marine Hospital is a two-story structure on a raised basement. It features a gabled central section with a lunette, tetrastyle one-story Doric portico, and flanking Tuscan colonnaded wings of five bays each. The Tuscan columns sit atop high brick pedestals, and the otherwise smooth shafted columns are fluted immediately below the capitals. Though some antebellum buildings display this odd juxtaposition, it could indicate that the capitals were purchased as stock items meant to match fluted shafts. To save money, Bunnell might have avoided buying the fluted shafts, or taking the time and trouble to fashion them on-site, and instead had smooth shafts erected. Barnes might have grumbled that that's what comes of taking the low bid!

Elsewhere downtown, Greek Revival expressions were more muted and occasionally grafted onto existing buildings in strange ways. Two examples will suffice. Around 1840 a man named John Nugent erected three buildings on Claiborne Street. Two of these have long since disappeared, but the surviving brick building, known locally as the Waring Texas House, still stands. The name derives from a subsequent owner, Moses Waring, who bought the property along with a fair portion of the block in 1868. Waring lived in a large two-story house fronting Government Street and used Nugent's little house as a *garçonnière*, or "Texas," so named because it was remote from the main dwelling and therefore a suitable domain for the family's raucous boys. Years later, a descendant claimed that the Texas had also served as a schoolhouse and its first story as a wine cellar.[15]

It is unknown whether or not the original builder had Carolina roots, but with its end gable to the street and flanking porch configuration, the Waring Texas strongly resembles a Charleston side house.[16] The Greek Revival influence is brought into full play on the attractive porch, with its boxed columns and trimmed out capitals supporting a light entablature. A balustrade with turned spindles deters anyone from tumbling off the high porch. Nicely proportioned large windows provide plenty of light and air to the interior. Heavy gates demarcate the property from Claiborne Street.

Another highly unusual example is the Jonathan Kirkbride House (also known as the Conde-Charlotte House and operated as a museum by the Colonial Dames) at 104 Theatre Street. Physical and documentary evidence confirms that this house was originally a jail, built in 1822 if not earlier and then extensively improved during the late 1840s by Kirkbride and Robert Ellis, who were, handily enough, master builders. Kirkbride's family occupied the home until 1926.[17]

Exactly what the jail might have looked like when Kirkbride and Ellis acquired it in 1849, and whether or not it had suffered any fire damage or been renovated in any way, is unknown. The New Orleans architect Samuel Wilson Jr. closely inspected the property during the mid-twentieth century and concluded that the first story was the older portion, with the second-story gallery and the east wing most likely added by Kirkbride and Ellis. In fact, the master builders may have been responsible for the entire second story. The building had one owner between its use as a jail and the Kirkbride/Ellis ownership, and this individual may have made improvements as well. The dichotomy in porch columns — heavy stuccoed brick Tuscan pillars at the first story and lighter wooden Corinthian columns with a crow's foot balustrade above — could have been either intentional or indicative of distinct phases of construction.[18] As it stands today, the Kirkbride House is an interesting mix of older trends and the

The Waring Texas (1840), 110 South Claiborne Street. Unabashedly urban and likely influenced by the Charleston side house tradition, this building presently serves as a den for a Mardi Gras mystic society.

Jonathan Kirkbride House. This building's evolution in the late 1840s from rude jail to pillared downtown landmark is one of the most unusual in local architectural history.

Greek Revival. Its thick first-story walls, classical porch, rear galleries, and walled courtyard provide tangible evidence of the diverse building methods and stylistic preferences of antebellum Mobile.

This flexible application of Greek Revival principles also obtained in the surrounding countryside, where several homeowners achieved good results—the Hardaways at Georgia Cottage; Michael Carlen on his sturdy Dauphin Way farmhouse; and William Dawson with his high-style Charleston-influenced home in Spring Hill. That the Greek Revival was proving so adaptable augured well for its continued popularity, even as the available stylistic choices expanded.

During the 1840s, Mobile's city limits didn't extend much beyond Ann Street, and settlement was thin between there and the village of Spring Hill, some six miles west of downtown. Several primitive roads threaded out of town—Dauphin Way (now Dauphin Street) and the Spring Hill Road (today's Spring Hill Avenue)—and small farms and country retreats were established along their length. Georgia Cottage has already been examined, but there were others as early. Among these was the six-acre plot that Carlen purchased in 1842. The following year, Carlen took an Irish bride and built his house, which remained in the family until 1923.[19]

Long since swallowed into the city limits, the Carlen House stands out among its neighbors — modest bungalows and the Mission Revival–style Murphy High School — as a fine example of the Gulf Coast cottage type. Just as the Hardaways did at nearby Georgia Cottage, Carlen framed his house with heavy timbers, pegging them together at critical junctures with tree nails. Hand-split lath supports the interior plaster. But the Carlen House is more fully within the Gulf Coast cottage tradition than Georgia Cottage. The one-and-a-half story, five-bay frame dwelling rests on brick piers and features recessed full-length front and rear porches underneath the side-gabled roofline. The front porch is supported by heavy boxed columns with Tuscan Doric capitals, and the front entrance features a four-panel door flanked by simple pilasters with molded capitals and sidelights with a transom above. The interior plan consists of a central hall with, somewhat unusually, a reverse staircase, and two rooms to either side. Smaller upstairs rooms add to the living space, but considering that Carlen and his wife had nine children, conditions must have been tight on dreary winter days.

The Carlen House (1843) presents a good example of Greek Revival elements blended with the Gulf Coast cottage type. The surrounding farmland has long since been swallowed by the city's growth.

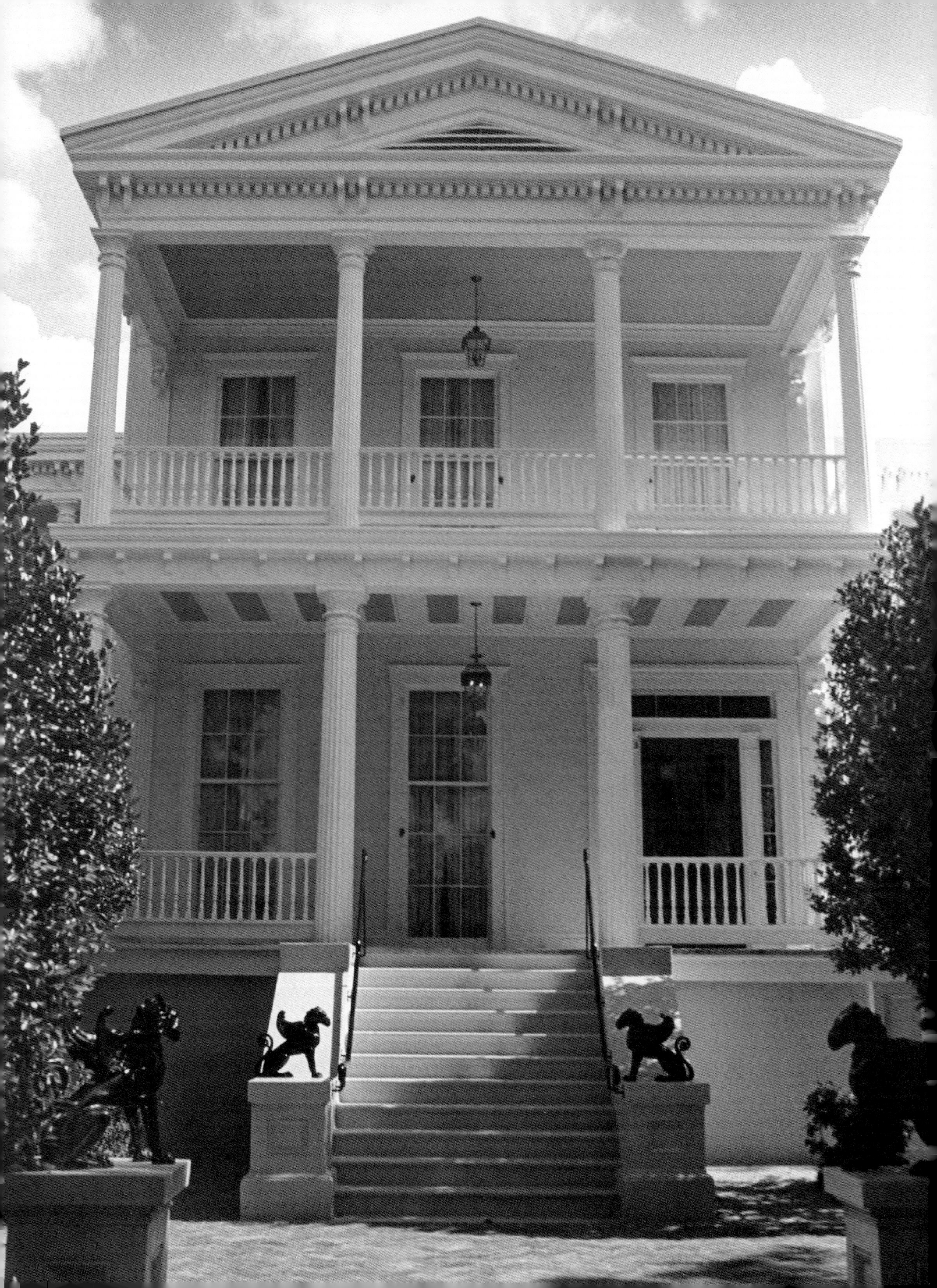

Spring Hill, more elevated than the marshy lowlands along the bay, developed during the early nineteenth century as an attractive and healthy retreat for the city's wealthy. Among those who settled here was a cotton factor and former Charleston resident named William Dawson. In 1845 Dawson erected a two-story home that was strongly reminiscent of the Georgian-style houses of his native city. Named, appropriately enough, Carolina Hall, the house displays a stunning range of exterior and interior classical elements, all beautifully realized.

The house is a three-bay structure with a side-hall entrance and a pair of flanking rear wings. Two-story recessed porches grace the facade and wings, all supported by columns copied from the Tower of the Winds. Decorative balustrades, denticulated cornices with delicate paired brackets, and a triangular louvered vent in the front gable all combine to produce a wedding-cake aspect.

The interior includes exquisitely detailed plasterwork ceiling medallions, crown molding with acanthus leaf and egg-and-dart patterns, eared architrave door surrounds, decorative panels above the parlor doors, and fluted pilasters and columns between the double parlors. A Gothic-style staircase dates from the 1880s. According to a bit of 1950s Old South mythmaking, fifteen house slaves maintained the interior in Dawson's day. In actuality, the 1850 slave schedule

(Opposite) Carolina Hall (1845), one of Mobile's best-preserved Greek Revival homes, is located in Spring Hill, several miles west of downtown. The hilltop was a popular nineteenth-century retreat among the Port City's elites.

(Below) Porch detail, Carolina Hall. These column capitals, like those supporting the balcony of Government Street Presbyterian Church, are copied from the Tower of the Winds.

lists only six, three of whom were small children, hardly likely to have been entrusted with a feather duster around the family china. The other three were an older couple and a twenty-year-old woman, all of whom likely did house and yard work.[20]

In the decade leading up to the Civil War, Mobile at last revived. Cotton exports increased from approximately 375,000 bales in 1849 to more than 600,000 bales by 1856. Just four years later, the city was the third busiest port in the nation behind New York and New Orleans but well ahead of Charleston and Savannah.[21] The population approached thirty thousand residents, nearly a third of them foreign-born.[22] Civic boosters pushed railroad projects, and construction accelerated. In 1852 one Mobile businessman wrote to a judge, "You will scarcely know Mobile on your return, so great will be the changes and improvements." Among those he noted were the new five-story Battle House Hotel and several "fine, large brick stores."[23]

The early 1850s also saw the long-awaited completion of two monumental pillared edifices and the commissioning and construction of a third, the latter representing the most important Greek Revival project since the Marine Hospital ten years before.

In 1850 Portier and Beroujon at last finished the new cathedral. Much relieved, Portier wrote to the Bishop of New Orleans, "Everybody says that my church is worthy of its object, and I believe for my part, especially after twelve years of work and worry, that I accomplished my mission." The local press was suitably awed and displayed considerable architectural knowledge in its description of the new edifice: "All the outside projections are of granite — the water-table, the bases of all the pilasters and columns, the neck-molding, the capitals, those that divide the architrave and frieze, and upper side of the cornice." Overall, the writer thought the end result presented a "chaste and beautiful appearance."[24]

Christ Church wasn't far behind and in May 1852 finally got its finish coat of stucco. The *Mobile Daily Register* reported: "This truly elegant structure is now about to be completed, the plasterers being very busy in putting a new face to matters (and bricks) on the outside. It has long been a source of much regret that a building of such really chaste design, and proportions should remain so unsightly. It more resembled the uncouth oyster rather than the apples of the dead sea — but now all within, and without, will soon be rendered spotless and elegant alike."[25]

The new project was a commission to replace Hobart and Judson's 1825 courthouse, which burned in October 1851. William Alderson was chosen as the architect, and on March 2, 1853, the *Mobile Daily Register* printed a contractors' solicitation. Interested parties were to submit sealed proposals with "bids for the whole" broken down to reflect "the different Artificers Work." Alderson was to receive bids at his upstairs Dauphin Street office through month's end between the hours of 9 a.m. to 1 p.m. and 3 to 6 p.m.[26] Based on this evidence, Alderson's work day corresponded closely to that of modern professional architects, though the latter might envy the apparent two-hour lunch.

With better luck than he had on the Marine Hospital bid, Barnes submitted the winning entry, which came in at $70,289. Like its predecessor, the new courthouse was to be a classically inspired building. Though there are no known photographs or good representations of the structure, the contract is specific enough to allow an overall grasp of the design. Since the building was to be brick covered in stucco, considerable attention was devoted to the quality and variety of the bricks themselves. According to the construction document, "Accurate working drawings will be furnished for the bricks necessary for the triglyphs and pilasters." From this clue, it may be concluded that the new courthouse was a more purely Greek Revival building than Hobart and Judson's earlier product. The contract also emphasized that "all the front and side columns and pilasters are to be built solid and firmly beded to be perfectly straight and round." There were numerous specifications for brick masons, stonemasons, roofers, plasterers, carpenters, and a coppersmith since the building was to have copper gutters. The finished building must have been handsome indeed — three stories, stuccoed, columned porticoes, full entablature, steps and trim in white marble, and the water table, column bases, and capitals in Tennessee blue marble.[27]

Despite these imposing additions to Mobile's skyline, travelers' impressions during the 1850s ran the gamut and were often colored by the individual's opinions on the increasingly contentious issue of slavery. This was certainly the case with the great landscape architect Frederick Law Olmstead, who passed through Mobile around 1853. Olmstead considered slavery to be morally reprehensible and any society that tolerated it correspondingly tainted. Not surprisingly, he found Mobile "dirty, and noisy, with little elegance, or evidence of taste or public spirit, in its people." Bienville Square, today the lovely, shaded heart of downtown, failed to impress the future designer of New York's Central Park. Olmstead stated that it was the only public open space in evidence and, rather than serving as an island of repose amid the urban bustle, was "used as a horse and hog pasture, and cloths drying-yard."[28]

About the same time, a woman visiting from Maine was troubled by the uncomfortable social contrasts she discovered but charmed by the soft climate and abundant flowers. "Everything looks strange," she wrote in her diary. "Went out alone in the morning, to see what I could see and do some shopping. The poor blacks meet me at every turn and I have many thoughts which perhaps had better remain unwritten. The air is like summer, the houses are all open and families sitting on their piazzas. Roses of many varieties are in bloom, also hyacinths, the orange tree and cape jasmine are clad in rich foliage together with a great variety of evergreen."[29]

Others had unreservedly positive reactions. Fredrika Bremer, a Swedish novelist who visited early in the decade, was completely enchanted by the city. "I like Mobile, and the people of Mobile, and the weather of Mobile, and everything in Mobile; I flourish in Mobile," she enthused.[30] John W. Oldmixon, the Englishman who had earlier thrilled to all of Philadelphia's white marble, was equally beguiled. Government Street, downtown's principal thoroughfare, was among the first things he noticed. In an era when many cities had brick, or cobblestone, or some other similarly rough paving, if any, Mobile's wide, sandy Government Street was amazingly easy on the traveler. "Carriages and light wagons fly through the streets as if on air," Oldmixon marveled, "for the sand is so soft, no noise is heard." Oldmixon estimated that these conveyances achieved speeds of an astonishing twelve to fifteen miles an hour.[31]

Of all the travelers to comment on Mobile during the 1850s, Oldmixon was the most attuned to architecture. "Except a few streets next the bay," he wrote, "and two or three central ones of half a mile in length, the whole town is in wood — wooden mansions, with noble columns and porticos, many of them. Columns, porticos, rich cornices, handsome verandahs meet the eye everywhere; it is a city of villas, the upper part standing in their own small gardens."[32]

With Mobile's increased growth and prosperity, the building trades once again prospered, and homeowners enjoyed a broader array of options in furniture, hardware, carpets, and fine things. In 1859 the city directory listed two architects (Alderson and T. S. James), eight builders, three painters, one slater, and two

Franklin Street Sabbath School Picnic, 1856, from a stereoscopic card. The exact location can no longer be determined, but the image presents a rare outdoor study of antebellum Mobilians enjoying their architecture. (Courtesy University of South Alabama Archives.)

tin and sheet-ironworkers.[33] The 1860 census tabulated even more builders — forty-three white males and twenty-four free black males. Furthermore, according to census data, more than sixty men labored in three lumberyards, thirty in the lone marble yard, and four specialized in plaster ornaments. The lumberyards supplied both sawed and planed wood, and the marble yard carried good mantelpieces, pavers, sills, lintels, and thresholds.[34] Three foundries dealt in ornamental and structural ironwork. George Elsworth & Co. advertised hardware and "carpenter's and tinner's tools." Dade, Hurxthal & Co., "Mobile Iron Store" on Water Street, dealt in bar iron, nails, and castings. Charles McCord, an upholsterer and paperhanger, declared that he was "at all times prepared to make carpets, curtains and hang paper." Allen's Furniture Ware-Rooms nearby advertised carpets, oilcloths, feather mattresses, bedroom and parlor sets, bedsteads, bureaus, wardrobes, bookcases, chairs, sofas, tables, and "tête-à-têtes."[35]

Besides the established merchants, there were itinerant salesmen, some of whom catered to the carriage trade. In March 1850, Signor Vito Viti & Sons took out a newspaper ad trumpeting a wide range of antiques and quality knick-knacks freshly acquired in Europe. The collection on offer, "carefully selected by the refined taste of Signor Vito Viti," was on display at the Armory Hall and included a patented shower bath, china cigar holders, engraved flower vases, fire screens, plated ware, tea urns, chocolate cups, marble statues, and mother-of-pearl work tables.[36]

As a flourishing seaport, Mobile had profound cultural influence on the Alabama and Mississippi interior. Up-country planters routinely visited, and besides paying calls on their factors, they stayed in the hotels, sampled oysters and other exotic fare, shopped in the stores, and took in the sights. Their wives and children sometimes accompanied them, absorbing cosmopolitan tastes in architecture, interior décor, and fashion. Some Mobile tradesmen found gainful employment with these planters, who were eager to replicate at home what they had seen on their trips south. Thus Greek Revival trends like the distyle in antis appeared on Black Belt churches, and decorative ironwork, marble mantelpieces, and other architectural elements ordered through the Port City wound up in houses far from the coast. In 1858 Col. George H. Young built a landmark Greek Revival home named Waverly near Columbus, Mississippi. Young contracted with at least three Mobilians to execute his ornamental marble and plasterwork on-site.[37]

For those builders disinclined to travel, plenty of work could be had closer to home. Numerous 1850s Greek Revival buildings survive in town and the adjacent countryside, and taken together provide an instructive sample of the style's range before the Civil War disrupted everything. In most cases, the identity

The Washington Number 5 Firehouse (1851) demonstrates the versatility of the Greek Revival style. The in antis pillars were adequately spaced so as to admit the wagons on the ground floor, while the firemen's living quarters were on the second story. The one-story wing to the left served as a machine shop and stable.

of who exactly designed or worked on which building can no longer be determined, but the quality of the workmanship nonetheless commands respect.

Among the most interesting of these structures is the old Washington Number 8 firehouse at 7 North Hamilton Street downtown. This fire company was founded in 1843, and in 1851 bought a lot and erected its headquarters at a cost of $5,500. The original architect or builder is unknown, but the Washington Number 8 (renamed Number 5 during the 1880s) is a beautifully proportioned, sophisticated, and yet completely practical and functional Greek Revival structure. Though hardly monumental in scale, its strong classical facade, featuring a pair of Doric columns in antis at the first floor, four pilasters contrasting with the red brick at the second floor, and pedimented gable above, certainly conveys an impression of solidity and taste. The original interior consisted of one large room downstairs with supporting cast iron columns, where the engine (nicknamed the "Lady Washington") was stored. Three sets of large double wooden doors provided quick and easy access to the street. The horses were kept in one-story sheds at the rear and on the south side. The second story featured a large open room with eared architrave window surrounds. This floor doubled nicely as a space for the firemen's numerous social events, including an annual ball. Surely whenever the alarm sounded and the company's members poured out of their handsome firehouse in their snappy red and white uniforms, Mobilians must have felt a surge of pride and confidence that the horrors of 1827 and 1839 would not be repeated.[38]

Smaller-scale Doric columns are also effectively employed on the Roberts-Abbot House at 910 Government Street. This two-story frame residence was constructed in 1855 by Joel and Mary Roberts. For their dwelling, the Roberts couple preferred a side-hall plan and two-story porch, eschewing the central-hall plan with full monumental portico popular upstate. The former was a typical preference in antebellum Mobile, as seen at Oakleigh, Carolina Hall, and others long since demolished. Interestingly, during the Civil War Roberts served as secretary and treasurer of the Mechanics Aid Association.[39]

Closer to the river, where space was limited and construction denser, brick town houses and row houses were the rule. These were either plain with Greek Revival embellishments, as on the Parmly House at 307 North Conception Street, or more forcefully Grecian like the Ravesies House at 401 Church Street.

The Roberts-Abbot House (1855) is one of the oldest homes on Government Street. Its two-story Doric porch was a favorite local variant of the Greek Revival.

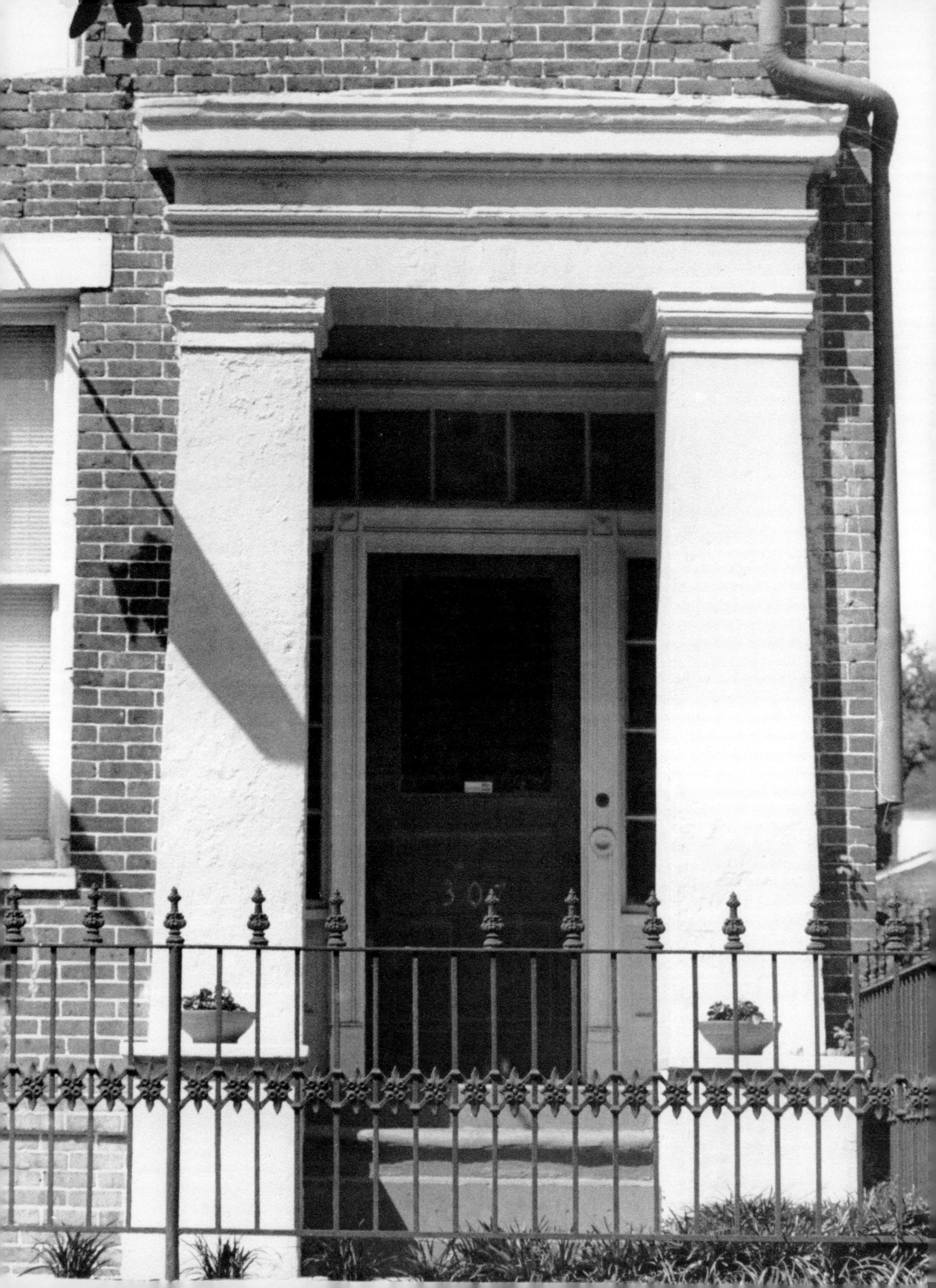

The Parmly House is a three-story brick side-hall residence with a heavy Greek Revival doorway. Erected in 1852 by a dentist named Ludolph Parmly, this house displays the larger scale and bulkier accents of the 1850s and vividly contrasts with the adjoining, plainer, two-story row houses dating from 1842.[40]

The Ravesies House was built in 1860 by Frederick P. Ravesies, a cotton broker and the son of one of the early nineteenth-century French settlers who started the Vine and Olive colony north of Mobile. He subsequently deeded the property to his wife, Isabella, "feeling the obligation of providing a permanent home."[41] Unlike the Parmly House, the Ravesies House more fully employs a Greek Revival vocabulary, evidenced by the recessed classical side-hall entry and its heavy exterior surround, a projecting denticulated cornice, and the broken, paneled parapet above.

(Opposite) Detail, Parmly House entrance (1852). Because of the general heaviness of execution and battered (sloping) sides, these doorways are frequently, and erroneously, labeled as Egyptian. But they are typical of the Greek Revival style and are commonly found on both interiors and exteriors.

(Left) Detail, Ravesies House (1860). Live oak limbs foreground this Greek Revival town house, creating a coastal/classical juxtaposition not uncommon in Alabama's seaport.

The Roberts-Staples House (1851) is situated on one of Mobile's most spacious lots. Framed by azalea bushes, live oaks, and swaying Spanish moss, it is the quintessential Gulf Coast home.

Greek Revival–modified Gulf Coast cottages like the Carlen House came fully into their own during the 1850s and were built everywhere — downtown, Spring Hill, and the Eastern Shore. Among the finest to survive are the Roberts-Staples House at 1614 Old Shell Road in Mobile and the Captain Adams-Stone House on Captain O'Neal Drive in Daphne, overlooking Mobile Bay. Both of these residences are typical of the style, albeit somewhat grander and better appointed than average. Each of them rests on brick piers and has a five-bay facade, central entrance, side-gabled roof with recessed porch supported on bulky boxed columns with bases and capitals, and a trio of pedimented dormers.

Joel Roberts built the Roberts-Staples House in 1851, several years before his house on Government Street. Within a year, Roberts sold the property to Mary Jane Calef. That he was the builder, however, is confirmed by the 1852 tax record, which lists a "frame house and land" in his name on the Shell Road, valued at two thousand dollars, a realistic figure for a dwelling of that size.[42]

Throughout the nineteenth century, Mobile's elites summered on the Eastern Shore, savoring the high bluffs and cooling breezes. Many built homes and moved their families over to escape the torpor and yellow fever fears that prevailed in downtown Mobile during the warm months. Come fall, the houses were shuttered or less frequently visited. Since one could cross the bay by steamer in only about two hours, the Eastern Shore was an easily accessible destination, and some men actually spent a portion of the working day in town, recrossing the bay in the evening.

The Captain Adams-Stone House was built in 1850 by James J. Adams, skipper of the steamboat *Cahawba*. His home has the distinction of being the only area Greek Revival house to host a United States president. On April 17, 1854, the *Alabama Planter* described a triumphal tour by Millard Fillmore, just out of office, and an accompanying delegation. The purpose of the trip, according to the paper, was to "give the gentlemen . . . an opportunity to see the beautiful region known as the Eastern Shore." The party assembled aboard "the fine little steamer *Junior*," brightly decorated "with gay streamers and fluttering flags," and departed the Mobile wharf for Baldwin County. After receiving a salute midpassage from a U.S. Navy cutter, the *Junior* docked at the head of the bay, and the distinguished tourists worked their way south, visiting prominent citizens, speechifying, and receiving homage. The newspaper reported that the president's path was "literally strewn with flowers." About halfway through the tour, the party ascended Captain Adams's flower-bedecked gallery with its sweeping bay view, and "besides other good things, old style Virginia juleps were served in profusion."[43]

In Spring Hill, on the opposite side of the city, more formal Greek Revival residences were built. Of these, Stewartfield and the Marshall-Dixon House are among the best, the former notable for its ballroom and oak allée, and the latter for its low-slung villa-like character and intact antebellum gardens.

Stewartfield was built in 1850 by a twenty-eight-year-old cotton factor named Roger Stewart. Oral tradition long maintained that the house was named for his ancestral Scottish estate, but this is a fiction. It was not called Stewartfield until after 1940, the name deriving from a combination of his surname and that of a family member, Anna Field, who later occupied the house.[44]

Stewart clearly had panache, however, and his home impressed locals and visitors alike. The property included a large oval racetrack out front, pierced by the long oak allée that led to the house itself. This unusual but highly satisfactory arrangement allowed guests to leisurely watch the horses from the comfort of the porch's wicker rockers. One man whose father frequented the place in antebellum

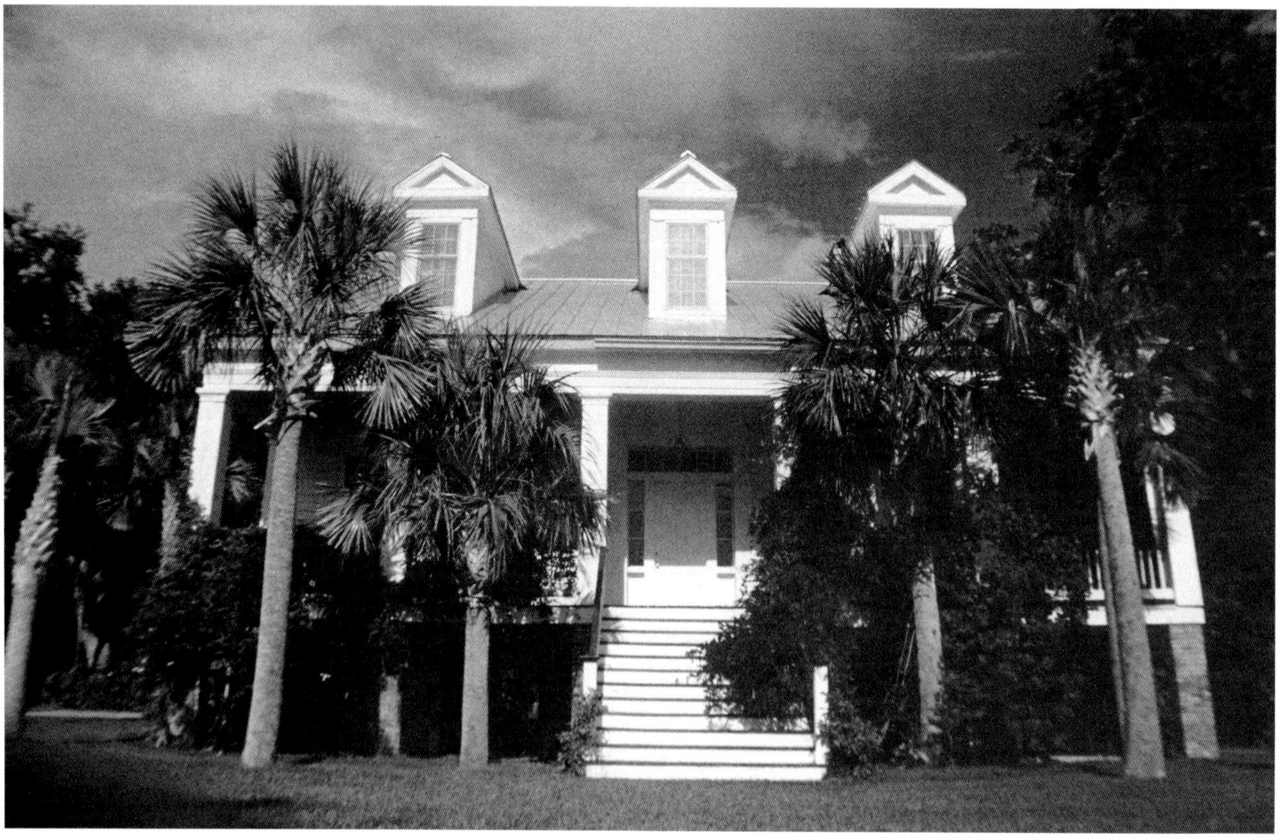

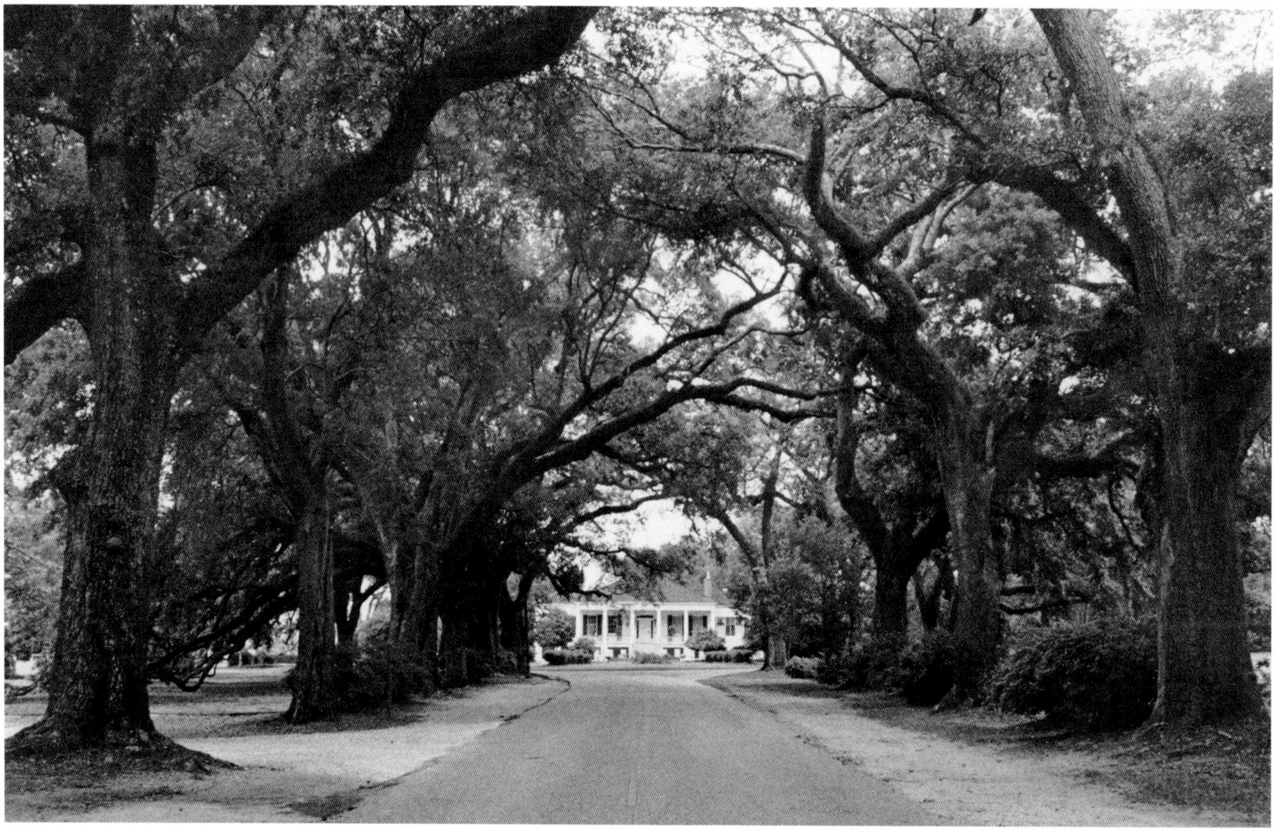

years described an "aristocratic formality and lavish hospitality" defined by elaborate dinner parties where guests wore white kid gloves and danced the Virginia reel.[45] A young woman who visited in 1852 was awed, writing in her diary, "We went to his bath house and from there to his ten pin alley where we amused ourselves. . . . They live in great style and have their home beautifully furnished."[46]

Today Stewartfield is owned and maintained by Spring Hill College and looks much as it did in its antebellum heyday. Set well back from Old Shell Road at the end of its allée, Stewartfield is a pleasing Greek Revival country cottage with a low hip roof, recessed porch supported by Doric columns, flush board facade, eared architrave central entrance, jibbed windows, and, of course, the rear half-circle ballroom, specially underpinned to allow it to spring beneath the dancers' weight.

Not far from Stewartfield is the Marshall-Dixon House at 152 Tuthill Lane. Built around 1853 by a South Carolina–born cotton factor named Benjamin Franklin Marshall, the house represents the Greek Revival's local apogee as refined country dwelling. The house sits in the midst of a five-acre square, surrounded by its original landscaping laid out by Mrs. Marshall, a surveyor, and an old German gardener. The landscape features include a pair of iron entrance gates, a circular driveway with a fountain and urn in the center, and flanking propeller-shaped walkways bordered by large camellia bushes.[47] In the 1930s, when the property was surveyed and drawn by the Historic American Buildings Survey, one of the

(Opposite, top) The Captain Adams-Stone House (1850), situated on the Eastern Shore, is the finest example of a Gulf Coast cottage in the bay area. Its Greek Revival embellishments include the boxed columns, formal central entrance, and classically framed dormers. The house commands a magnificent bay view.

(Opposite, bottom) Situated at the end of its avenue of oaks, Stewartfield (1850) has long been one of the city's loveliest historic sites.

Stewartfield is a fine example of a Greek Revival country house with its raised foundation, Doric columns, balanced facade, and matching chimneys.

(Right) Detail, front parlor window, Stewartfield. The utility of the jibbed window is readily apparent in this view.

(Below) Detail, ceiling medallion, Stewartfield. These kinds of plaster ornaments help break up expanses of white space. The acanthus leaf motif is common for the period.

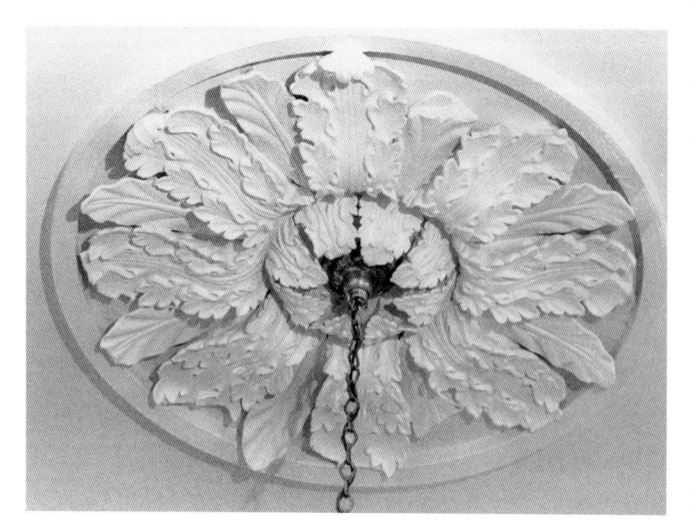

(Right) Exterior view, Stewartfield's rear ballroom. This unusual amenity was the talk of antebellum Mobile's social set and a marvel of design and workmanship.

Interior, Stewart-field ballroom. The dedication of so much square footage to entertainment astonished many Mobile residents before the Civil War.

Stewartfield's west parlors are handily divided by a pair of pocket doors that glide as smoothly along their way as the day they were installed.

team members wrote, "The garden plan delineates itself upon the draftsman's sheet in a way to warm the heart of him who is a landscape architect."[48]

The house itself rests on brick piers and has a low hip roof, even lower than that of Stewartfield. A recessed, balustraded front porch covers the width of the facade and is supported by Doric columns with a denticulated cornice above. The central entrance is flanked by Ionic colonettes, and the front windows are full-length six-over-nine panes. Flanking rear wings also have recessed porches and are accessed by semicircular steps. A centered, recessed back porch provides even more ventilation possibilities for the interior.

The wide central hall has a pair of parlors to either side. Interior details and appointments are altogether superior. Eared-architrave door and window surrounds display an exaggerated batter, giving them an even greater sense of height (the doorways are twelve feet high as it is, counting the transoms); wide louvered doors with four-inch slats divide the hallway in half; denticulated cornices decorate most rooms; and marble mantels, outsized mirrors, and crystal chandeliers complete the ensemble.

The Marshall-Dixon House (ca. 1853) is one of Mobile's most significant Greek Revival country houses. Its surrounding antebellum garden, anchored by the urn and stuccoed brick basin in front of the house, is an extraordinarily rare survival. Only a few remain in Alabama.

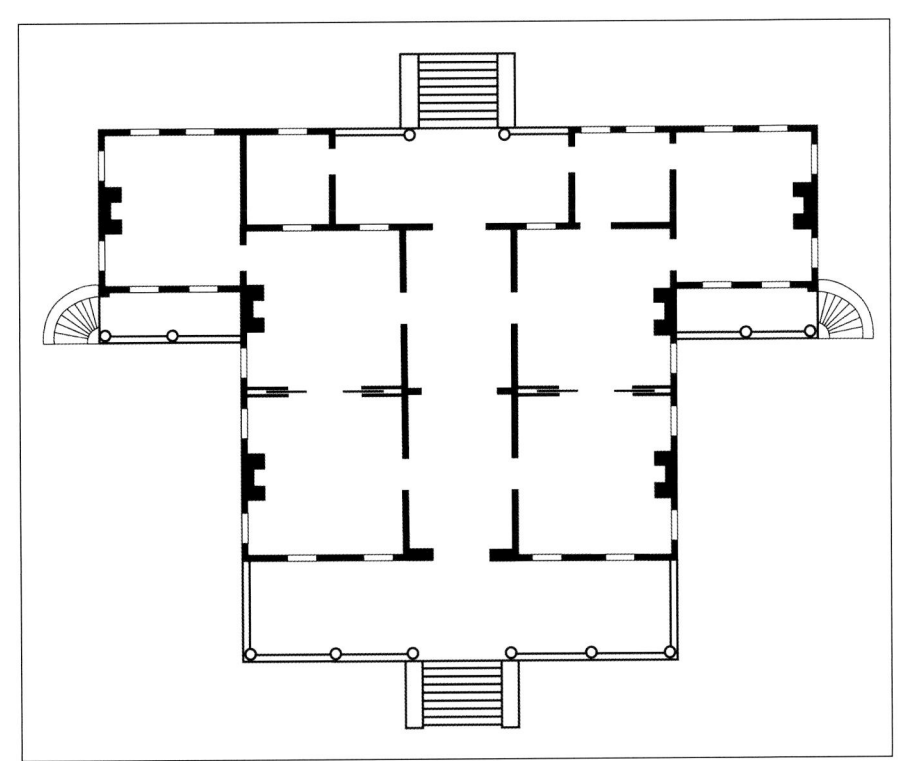

(Above, left) Front parlor, Marshall-Dixon House. The exaggerated eared-architrave surrounds positively soar in this room.

(Above, right) Detail, silver-plated doorknob and keyhole cover at the Marshall-Dixon House. Such appointments are found in only the finest Greek Revival houses. Might children, lovers, or slaves have once spied or whispered secrets here?

(Left) Floor plan, Marshall-Dixon House. The central hall arrangement is the general rule for Greek Revival country houses around the state.

The Bragg-Mitchell Mansion stands amid a gorgeous live oak grove northwest of downtown. This house is one of Mobile's most famous and is a stunning example of the bracketed Greek Revival that became popular just before the Civil War.

A final trend was manifested immediately before the Civil War when builders began accenting Greek Revival houses with Italianate details, especially eave brackets. Sometimes referred to as the "bracketed Greek Revival," this stylistic evolution proved particularly popular in the western reaches of the Black Belt, and two surviving Mobile homes also illustrate it to good effect.

The Bragg-Mitchell Mansion stands amid a spectacular live oak grove on the north side of Spring Hill Avenue. It was built around 1855 by a North Carolina native and judge named John Bragg. Bragg had moved to Mobile in 1835, hung out his shingle as a lawyer, and during the panic made a good living handling foreclosures. In 1842 he was appointed to the circuit court and five years later married Mary Frances Hall, herself wealthy and landed. During the early 1850s, he served a term in Congress and then returned to Mobile and built his mansion.[49]

At the time, the site was known as Summerville and represented a desirable suburban address for those who could afford it. Just who designed the mansion, one of Mobile's finest, is unknown, but there are several strong possibilities. To begin with, the judge's father had been a building contractor who worked on the North Carolina capitol in 1820, so he was presumably sensitive to the art. Secondly, Bragg's brother Alexander was talented in the trades and might have designed the house. Thomas James has also been listed as a possibility, as has Alderson, who was a close friend of Bragg's and who, of course, employed a Grecian vocabulary on the new courthouse.[50]

Whoever was responsible, their achievement was, like Oakleigh, an inspired blend of formal and informal with an eye to the climatic realities of the Gulf Coast. After a thorough analysis of the house, the prominent architectural historian William Seale wrote, "I know of no other domestic architectural composition assembled in quite this way, whimsy is a main ingredient in its charm." Seale particularly admired the character-defining, elongated slender columns, the bracketed cornice, high windows, and "delicate Romeo balcony fenced in cast iron."[51]

Like Oakleigh, the Bragg-Mitchell Mansion is also T-shaped, allowing for good cross ventilation, and features a side-hall plan. Unlike Oakleigh, however, the interior is palatial — fourteen rooms, sixteen-foot ceilings, a fifty-foot parlor broken by three arches supported on freestanding columns, and a wide, curving staircase out in the hall. Bragg's floor coverings and furnishings were suitably expensive — white velvet carpets embossed with pink flowers, carved rosewood parlor pieces upholstered in satin damask, and beds, chairs, and sofas imported from New York, Baltimore, and Philadelphia.[52]

In 1857 the wealthy landowner Joshua Kennedy Jr. erected his own impressive house much closer to the river on Government Street. According to at least one source, the house was a wedding present to Kennedy and his new bride, Mary Emanuel, from the latter's father, Jonathon Emanuel, whose own high-style Greek Revival home stood just a few blocks to the east.[53] In its design, however, the Kennedy House represents a strong blending of Italianate elements with classical precedent. The two-story stuccoed brick house is imposing, with its monumental Tuscan columns and flattened arches. Furthermore, its bracketed eaves, rounded windows and doors, and highly decorative interior flourishes like elaborately molded, hooded windows complete with broken pediments, drop pendants, and floral motifs are all much more redolent of the Italianate than the Greek Revival.

A fascinating portrait of what life was like in these houses immediately before the Civil War is provided by the charming book *A Little Boy in Confederate Mobile*, penned by Peter Joseph Hamilton late in life. Hamilton was a prominent lawyer and local historian during the late nineteenth century who grew up in a Greek Revival house on Government Street a bit west of Broad Street. In fact, his boyhood home, sadly long gone, closely resembled the Roberts-Abbot House.

In his account, Hamilton wrote of a happy, quiet life there, at least until the war came. He described a front yard "divided into flower beds and sheltered

The Kennedy House (1857) represents the transition from the Greek Revival style to the Italianate in the Gulf South. The flattened arches, rounded windows, and heavy eave brackets are all typical of the latter trend, while the full-height pillars preserve the local affection for classical architecture.

by oaks" and out back a cistern that gathered rainwater from the roof, a brick kitchen, servants' quarters, a well, a chicken yard, a washhouse, and a mix of fig trees, scuppernong arbors, and a vegetable garden.[54]

Like the Roberts-Abbot House, Hamilton's home had a side hall with double parlors that were furnished, he recalled, with "hair-covered furniture on which

I had difficulty in retaining my seat until I grew up enough for my feet to touch the floor." Even as a child he was impressed by the white marble mantels, but he wrote that the hall itself "had no warmth in winter." In the back study, a portrait of Daniel Webster hung over the mantel. Lee and Jackson would come later, Hamilton assured the reader, "but Webster was of interest to me because in the salutes over the secession of Alabama in 1861 he fell, breaking glass and frame."[55]

Unfortunately, the Hamilton family's Webster portrait wasn't the only thing that would be smashed in 1860s Mobile. But during the war's earliest months, the city seemed like a safe refuge, far enough removed from the action to escape serious damage. As the war progressed, considerable excitement was generated as Confederate troops camped about the city or traveled through by train, fearsome new vessels like the ironclad ram *Tennessee* and the submarine *Hunley* appeared in the river, and despite the blockade, daring captains slipped through and offered their wares to the local population.

Mobile's leading citizens responded to the conflict in different ways. Since many of them were from New England or abroad, they were acutely aware that a blockade would prove disastrous to their commercial interests. These interests were, after all, bound up with northern or foreign banks and offices, and those relationships stood to be interrupted or irrevocably broken. Others were strongly supportive of the cause. These included Judge Bragg, who helped draft the Confederate constitution and whose brother, Braxton, was an important Confederate general; and Benjamin Franklin Marshall, who invested heavily in bonds and, according to one account, even donated his copper roof to the Rebel navy.[56]

The members of Government Street Presbyterian Church also actively supported the Confederacy. They paid to equip forty soldiers, distributed religious literature among the troops, and bought bonds. Early in the war, the deacons assessed matters and were, on balance, thankful. "We feel like giving glory to God that our city is still unmolested," the session minutes recorded. "In our own church, the congregation have continued large and full in spite of many absent members."[57]

At Barton Academy, bored students welcomed all the commotion and distraction. Years later, a former pupil recalled her childhood excitement: "Some days in the quiet of the school hour, we would hear a bugle — then a drum beating — announcing a review on Government Street. We would all rush to the windows to watch our boys in grey as they were reviewed by some general."[58]

Most young men were indeed under arms, and those who were too old vociferously expressed their sentiments. Despite growing enthusiasm for the Confederacy, not everyone in town was a secessionist. There were a number of Union men, some prominent, none perhaps so vehement as Thomas James. Already

Augusta Evans Wilson, ca. 1870. The sadness of the war years is evident in her gentle eyes. (Courtesy of Larry Massey, University of South Alabama Archives.)

known for his argumentative streak, James got into a heated confrontation with an acquaintance in early April 1862, and things quickly turned ugly. His enraged adversary gripped him by the throat and snarled that he would make him swallow his words. Badly shaken and in poor health already, James beat a hasty retreat, took to his bed, and was dead within twenty-four hours.[59] It was an ignominious end for a man of his talents and accomplishments.

As the war advanced, nonmilitary building projects ceased. Money was tight, and those with construction or engineering experience were in high demand for survey and fortification work in all theaters. Even though Mobile escaped direct fighting, increasing numbers of casualties poured into the city — grim confirmation that things were going poorly. Barton Academy was pressed into service as a hospital (and probably many other buildings were as well).

Several large military encampments were also established around the city, including one close to Georgia Cottage named Camp Beulah in honor of one of Augusta Jane Evans's novels. In the summer of 1863, a Confederate soldier described it as "a lovely camp on a calm beautiful stream near some paper mills, just in the rear of the residence of Miss Augusta Evans." He added that since the camp was so close to the author's house, the name choice was obvious.[60]

For her part, Evans was an enthusiastic and tireless devotee of the southern cause. She conducted a prodigious correspondence with prominent Confederate political and military leaders, and she commandeered a small house near Georgia Cottage for a hospital. She wrote to one friend in the summer of 1863, "For two months past I have been constantly engaged in nursing sick soldiers, keeping sleepless vigil by day and night."[61]

Though there was economic hardship and human suffering to be sure, the city's buildings remained intact until late January 1864, when Alderson and Barnes's new courthouse mysteriously caught fire and burned. The blaze started in the attic and soon spread through the entire building. Fortunately the records were saved, but yet another pillared landmark was lost to fire. The *Mobile Commercial Register* jumped to the conclusion that it was "of course, a piece of incendiarism." The paper went even further and asserted that "the natural explanation, without seeking further, is that it is merely a part of the Yankee system for the gradual destruction of our city."[62]

Within two weeks, the building superintendent and acting sheriff, U. T. Cleveland, had investigated and felt compelled to offer his interpretation to the public. According to his published account, the likely cause was a flue that had been broken by settlement. Soot within the flue had apparently caught fire, and the flames shot through the crack and ignited rafters in the attic. Cleveland concluded that the blaze was likely "not the work of malice or design."[63]

The courthouse fire aside, visitors to the Port City during and right after the war were glad to see so little evidence of destruction. In late April 1864, a Confederate officer's wife named Frances Woolfolk Wallace spent several days in town and wrote: "What a beautiful city Mobile is, quite a feast to the eye, so many splendid residences. I think it the most beautiful place I have ever seen. . . . I would so much like to live here."[64] And early in 1865, on the eve of the Battle of Spanish Fort, a Confederate soldier marching through was pleased to find his hometown "not at all changed in appearance."[65]

After Mobile fell, some of the occupying Union troops were equally delighted. "The city itself, for beauty of architecture in its buildings and superior location will bear favorable comparison with any other of like dimensions," declared Lt. J. Wilkins Moore of the Twentieth Iowa. Moore rambled all over the city and found much to admire. "There are now about twenty places of worship," he wrote, "among them many church edifices which would be creditable to any city in the Union, whilst all are neat, well built, and well attended by — ladies." He also commented on the "large and commodious" hospital, presumably the City Hospital, and Barton Academy —"The architectural display in its facade and lofty dome makes it one of the chief ornaments of the city."[66]

Mobile's good fortune in escaping physical ruin came to an abrupt end on May 25, 1865, when a large powder magazine exploded north of downtown. Exactly what caused the blast was never clearly resolved, though it was almost certainly accidental. Tons of black powder and shells were stored along the waterfront, and a careless worker or an errant spark was likely to blame.

Young Hamilton recalled the event. "I was on top of the fence at the foot of the garden with my Mammy," he wrote, "talking to Henry . . . when we felt what I should from my tropical experience now call an earthquake, indeed two or more in succession and, as we looked fearfully toward the city, over it swept a black cloud, dividing in two in the wind."[67] Another witness described the cloud as "a writhing giant — gaunt and grim — poised in mid-air, from whose wondrous loins sprang bursting shells, flying timbers, bales of cotton, barrels of rosin, bars and sheets of iron, bricks, stones, wagons, horses, men, women, and children, commingled and mangled into one immense mass."[68]

Lieutenant Moore and his men rushed to a scene "agonizing beyond description." Hundreds were killed or injured. In desperation the soldiers helped pull victims from the rubble, "some with heads crushed, and some in such a condition as to present anything but the semblance of a human being." Fifty wounded were admitted to the City Hospital, and eighty-nine to the U.S. Marine Hospital, stretching frenzied medical staffs beyond their limits. According to Moore, even as they worked, fires raged all around and ammunition continued to explode, ships and steamers burned in the river, and cotton bales along the wharf.[69]

The magazine explosion leveled eight square blocks. Most of the destroyed buildings were warehouses, cotton presses, livery stables, and the like, since the heart of downtown was spared the direct blast. Still, virtually every structure within the city limits had some damage — stove-in doors, broken windows, and burned roofs caused by falling embers.[70] An Ohioan who surveyed the immediate aftermath found "houses shattered, bottom stories bereft of superstructure . . . gable-ends standing up alone, without the roofs they were raised to bear."[71] Portier reported to a fellow bishop, "Our cathedral suffered considerably all the windows on the side facing the explosion having been crushed in — sashes and glass." He was thankful that the building was empty at the time.[72]

For those who could remember, it must have seemed as bad as or worse than 1839 — a swath of the city a smoldering wreck, hundreds dead, the economy a disaster — and looming over all the gloomy prospect of military defeat and armed occupation. Mobile's residents faced decades of struggle and recovery. When the smoke cleared and building began again, Greek Revival was no longer the architectural style of choice. Even so, those pillared landmarks that remained soon exerted their irresistible allure and were extolled once more as the epitome of grandeur and taste.

EPILOGUE

THE LONG REVERBERATION

The Civil War was a great watershed in southern history, though there was more cultural continuity than is perhaps generally appreciated. In Mobile a few modest Greek Revival houses were built into the 1870s, Gulf Coast cottages through the 1880s, and two local homes — one near the Bragg mansion and the other in Spring Hill — were patterned after James Roper's Oakleigh. But for the most part, the Greek Revival style had run its course by 1865.

Mobilians during the latter half of the nineteenth century cheerfully embraced the myriad new architectural styles as they became popular but retained affection for classical elements and details. This may be seen in the 1880s Italianate town homes with two-story boxed columns, the 1890s Queen Anne cottages with Tuscan porch columns and dentil work, and the early 1900s neoclassical churches and houses with monumental, columned porticoes that gracefully line Government Street. By the turn of the century, in fact, Mobile was still very much a city of columns, though without the overwhelmingly Grecian ambience of antebellum years.

Many older pillared landmarks survived, of course, lending dignity and distinction to city streets. As the decades progressed, these buildings met with various fates — merciless fire, wanton demolition, gentle decay, and loving restoration. During the 1930s and 1940s, they began to be romanticized as symbols of Old South mystery and glamour, and were soon tourist destinations and objects of civic pride.

By the turn of yet another century, gifted young architects were once again consulting Asher Benjamin and Minard Lafever in an effort to build classically inspired and proportioned residences that would please a new breed of client, attuned to historical precedent and desirous of meaningful buildings. Classical details that hadn't been employed for a hundred years, like fluted Doric columns, acanthus leaves, and anthemions, were dusted off and placed on banks and houses all around the bay.

Of Mobile's four earliest pillared edifices — Hobart's courthouse, Roper's Oakleigh, George's City Hospital, and Beroujon's Spring Hill College — only two sur-

This modest Greek Revival cottage at 159 S. Dearborn Street was constructed in 1866. Its eared-architrave door and window surrounds seem almost squeezed under the porch. Classical amenities were quickly eclipsed by more popular Victorian gingerbread after the Civil War.

vive. The courthouse's destruction has already been detailed. Beroujon's Spring Hill College building, with its monumental, galleried portico and soaring cupola, was lost to fire on February 12, 1869. The building had stood for thirty-nine years and served as a combination museum, library, scientific laboratory, and men's dormitory. The blaze was discovered near midnight and quickly leapt out of control. According to a newspaper reporter on the scene, "The fire was very beautiful, great masses of smoke and flame mingling in their mad dance, whirling round the crumbling walls only to sweep them in their dreadful clasp and hurl them down broken and shattered."[1]

Another eyewitness described the event in painful detail. "It is deafening to listen to the crackling of the slates when the wood-lining to which they are fastened takes fire," he wrote. "Shortly the roof trembles and a column of sparks shoots high into the air, large tongues of flame issue in several places." Then came a series of loud rumbles, and the rafters broke, shearing off large sections of masonry as they collapsed into the building's heart. Amid the blackness appeared "a yawning mouth of fire which opened its jaws wider and wider."[2] College officials quickly rebuilt, but not in the Greek Revival style.

Many other Greek Revival landmarks disappeared in subsequent years — the Emanuel House, the reconstructed Planters and Merchants Bank, the Ottenstein House, and Hebron Palmer's handsome Unitarian Church. Added to the United States Hotel, the St. Michael Street Hotel, the first Planters and Merchants Bank, Hobart's 1825 courthouse, and Alderson's 1854 courthouse, this constitutes a singularly depressing catalog of lost landmarks for one city.

Despite this attrition, by the 1930s Mobile retained enough of an Old South ambience to inspire a talented cadre of local colorists. Their sketches, paintings, prose, and verse effectively conjured the romantic coastal flavor they experienced when contemplating the city's surviving historic architecture. Their work is of little scholarly value, since they were less interested in facts than atmosphere, but they did much to foster the historic preservation movement in its earliest days.

Marian Francis Acker, a former Mardi Gras queen and a Junior League founder who lived downtown, was one of the most capable. She was much taken with ornamental ironwork and early colonial architecture, but she also included illustrations of several Greek Revival buildings in her 1938 book *Etchings of Old Mobile*. Among these latter structures were the U.S. Marine Hospital, Barton Academy, and the Joshua Kennedy House, which was then a Seamen's Bethel.

The Emanuel House under demolition, 1936. Shredded curtains flutter from the second-story windows in sad elegy. Today the Admiral Semmes Hotel occupies the lot. (Courtesy Erik Overbey Collection, University of South Alabama Archives.)

Barton Academy, from an etching by Marian Acker, ca. 1932. In her accompanying text, Acker lauded the "atmosphere of peace and permanence in Old Barton." (Courtesy MAM Arts and the Estate of Marian A. MacPherson.)

Of the hospital she wrote, "A history of Time and Age is written in the creviced plaster of the walls and rains of bygone days have mellowed brick and stone."[3]

A few years later, in 1946, Mary Randelette Beck published *Ghosts of Old Mobile*, which featured short poems alongside illustrations of local landmarks. For the Kirkbride House she wrote, "The Grecian pillars tower to tell in stately pride/That past distinction, charm, and power endure at Old Kirkbride."[4]

Even as Beck was crafting her book, Mobile painter Genevieve Southerland, a founder of the Alabama Gulf Coast Art Colony, produced a watercolor of Georgia Cottage. Like many artists and tourists, she was just as enamored of the flowers and trees as she was of the architecture. "It has been my pleasure to paint some of the beauties which surround Georgia Cottage," she wrote, "the moss-hung oaks, flowers from the formal garden, magnolias, camellias, roses and lilies, the old house, set in the midst of all this beauty — the charm of soft sunlight dappled on century old trees and emerald lawns." What she most hoped to convey though, was "some thrill from the days of the Golden Age."[5]

Over the course of the twentieth century the city managed to effectively capitalize on this fascination and developed a robust tourist trade. In 1929 the Azalea Trail was inaugurated. Sponsored in part by the chamber of commerce, this fifteen-mile trail brought tens of thousands of tourists into town every February/March when the azaleas peaked. A successful homes tour was soon established as well, and continues to this day.[6]

Three of Mobile's four historic house museums are important Greek Revival buildings — Oakleigh, the Bragg-Mitchell Mansion, and the Kirkbride House — and have much to do with public perception of the city. Oakleigh remained a private residence until the end of World War II. The Harold Seibert

Mobile belles repose on the steps of the McClure House at 2104 Old Shell Road, while a guide stands just inside the screen door, ca. 1940. The juxtaposition of Confederate flags, hoopskirts, and Greek Revival architecture remains a widespread ritual throughout the South. Such associations did the McClure House little good, however, as it was demolished within a decade of this photograph. (Courtesy S. Blake McNeely Collection, University of South Alabama Archives.)

Denniston family owned the property from 1927 to 1945 and made several important changes during their stewardship. These included converting the ground floor into livable space, installing an interior staircase (a godsend to modern tour guides), and stuccoing the exterior brick. The Dennistons sold the house, appropriately enough, to the Hellenic American Progressive Association, and several other sales followed until the house was deeded to the City of Mobile in July 1955. The city then leased the structure to the Historic Mobile Preservation Society, which continues to operate it as a historic house museum.[7]

Still shot from a 1966 Borden's television commercial that employed a fully restored antebellum milk wagon with Oakleigh as a backdrop. The commercial aired throughout the Southeast. Mobile's Greek Revival landmarks have long served as popular settings for commercial as well as personal photographs. (Courtesy Historic Mobile Preservation Society.)

In 1931 Alfred and Minnie Mitchell bought the Bragg mansion. Minnie Mitchell devoted herself to gardening and historic restoration, planting azaleas and hydrangeas, and filling the house with antiques acquired in New Orleans. In November 1939 *House and Garden* magazine featured the mansion in a special *Gone with the Wind* issue. Thereafter, the Bragg-Mitchell Mansion became a staple of coffee-table books and magazine articles extolling southern architecture and gardens. Minnie Mitchell graciously showed the house to curious tourists. In the spring of 1947, a California man asked her, "Did you know that this is the most famous and respected, most antebellum house in the South?"[8]

After the Mitchells' deaths in the 1960s, the house was held by the family foundation until it was sold to the Exploreum for a science museum in 1983. Because the large frame residence was unsuitable to that purpose, the Exploreum constructed a new facility next door and in 1986 restored the mansion as a house museum.[9] Today the Bragg-Mitchell Mansion is especially popular for large weddings. On October 15, 2006, a bridal fashion show on the grounds drew 140 vendors, 145 brides-to-be, and more than 2,500 guests. The house's website has advertised its suitability for weddings with a series of photographs showing tuxedoed grooms and their gorgeous brides in carriages or sweeping down the staircase, accompanied by the *Gone with the Wind* theme music.[10]

The Kirkbride House was acquired and restored by the Historic Mobile Preservation Society in 1940. Seventeen years later the National Society of the Colonial Dames of America purchased the house for a museum. The Dames chose to devote each room to a different era of the city's history. According to an early brochure, "The Confederate room is furnished in the fashion of southern parlors at the outbreak of the War Between the States." The house was added to the National Register of Historic Places in 1973.[11]

The city's surviving pillared public buildings mostly fared well during the mid- to late twentieth century. The cathedral was beautifully restored in 2004, its exterior brick repointed and cleaned, and its interior barrel-vaulted ceiling ornately decorated. Christ Church lost its steeple during the hurricane of 1906 but was lovingly restored (with triglyphs, metopes, and guttae, which the original design had lacked, added) and still serves its congregation. Government Street Presbyterian Church was sympathetically enlarged at the rear in 1905 and again in 1916, and various minor interior changes have been made over the years. But overall, inside and out, it still looks very much as it must have when Charles Dakin married there in 1837.

The old Mobile City Hospital was likewise enlarged when the wings were extended after the turn of the century, but the building retains its original exterior character. The hospital staff was moved out in 1965 and the building placed on the National Register of Historic Places a year later. In the mid-1970s it was successfully restored as offices for the Mobile County Department of Pensions and Securities. The total restoration cost was $1.7 million. During the work, the architects and contractors were astonished to discover that Collins had built the structure without any kind of foundation. In an effort to provide better support, contractors carefully undergirded the walls with short sections of concrete, laid down four feet at a time to avoid weakening the structure.[12]

The U.S. Marine Hospital remained in use until 1955, when it was converted into a 170-bed tuberculosis hospital. In 1974 it closed, and the building was bought by the Mobile County Health Department for a headquarters and fully restored shortly thereafter. It is currently listed on the National Register of Historic Places, and despite some modification and new rear additions, it still presents an impressive Greek Revival facade to the street.[13]

Lastly, Barton Academy, Hitchcock's glory and the repository of so many community hopes and dreams, was unfortunately to become one of Mobile's most abused historic buildings.

For the first century it was well cared for, however. In fact, during Barton's centennial in 1936, "throngs of loyal alumni and faculty members" turned out to celebrate the grand institution.[14] But as the century progressed and the school system grew, maintenance of the old building became more of an issue.

The preservation architect. Nicholas Holmes Jr. poses at the Bragg-Mitchell Mansion, 1991. Over an astonishing half-century career, Holmes has helped restore many prominent Greek Revival landmarks in Alabama — including the state capitol, Sturdivant Hall in Selma, Christ Episcopal Church, and the Carlen House. He was also involved with the last significant repairs at Barton Academy in 1969.

The place had become so neglected by the spring of 1963 that Gov. George C. Wallace wrote to the *Mobile Register*, "It is my hope that your city will find it possible to preserve this historical landmark."[15] Suitably chastened, the Mobile County School Board allocated $50,000 for restoration in its 1964 budget.[16] Barton was no longer adequate for instructional purposes, however, and in 1965 was emptied of students and converted into administrative offices.

By the late 1960s the major work could no longer be put off. The cupola's wooden supports had begun to rot, and the entire drum had sunk some six inches into the main building. But the decision to thoroughly renovate, to the tune of almost two million dollars, unleashed the kind of public criticism that would make Barton's physical maintenance a politically dicey prospect for the rest of the century. "Who made the decision that spending $1,800,000 for renovation of Barton Academy was more beneficial than spending this money for construction of classrooms?" asked one outraged citizen. The board defended its decision, countering that restoration was cheaper than a new building, but the subsequent repairs would be the last for the foreseeable future.[17]

As the Mobile public school system, the largest in the state, struggled with the seemingly intractable problems of underachievement, student crime, and sprawling, high-maintenance buildings all over the county, Barton's deterioration continued apace. The school board and administrators, discredited in many peoples' eyes, were helpless to affect any repairs. The glum joke in Barton's halls was that even using borrowed paint and volunteer labor on a Saturday would provoke a public firestorm.

At the dawn of the millennium, Barton was an eyesore even to the casual observer. Its rotunda visibly listed, the Ionic columns on the lantern had mostly fallen away, a broken window was clumsily boarded, and during windstorms portions of the building crashed to the ground. After forty years without a paint job, both the edifice and the fence looked neglected and forlorn. In 2005 the Alabama Historical Commission and the Alabama Trust for Historic Preservation placed the building on its Places in Peril list. Local novelist Franklin Daugherty penned an angry article that summer titled "The Disgrace of Barton" for *Mobile Bay Monthly Magazine* that summed up the situation for frustrated preservationists. "Do the members of the Mobile County School Board care what happens to Barton Academy?" he asked. "The Greek and Roman portico, pediment, pilasters, Ionic columns, entablature and dome surmounted by a lantern . . . are invisible to them."[18]

In a gambit to try to save the venerable landmark, the Mobile Historic Development Commission and the Historic Mobile Preservation Society joined forces. Monies for a structural report were obtained and an architectural firm hired to do the study. A public awareness campaign and fund-raising efforts were also

The new classicists. Attorney and arbiter elegantiae *Palmer C. Hamilton (left) and architect Douglas Burtu Kearley enjoy their handiwork at 300 Marine Street. These men's adherence to good nineteenth-century design principles has helped reinvigorate one of the city's most important historic districts.*

launched, but when the beleaguered school administrative staff abandoned the building for new quarters west of downtown, some feared that all these efforts would come to naught. As of this writing, the outcome remains very much in doubt.[19]

Elsewhere, Greek Revival principles once again came into play for new construction. Under the leadership of local attorney Palmer C. Hamilton, federal monies were obtained to provide infill construction in Mobile's downtown historic districts. Hamilton procured the services of Mobile architect Douglas Burtu Kearley to design the new houses, most of which were built along Marine Street. Kearley, who had played around the Marshall-Dixon House as a child, harbored a profound respect for historic architecture in general and the Greek Revival in particular. "Classical architecture offers the opportunity to design buildings and places that are welcoming, well-proportioned, functional, rational, and visually satisfying," he explained. "By designing in a classical vein it is possible to create and provide a comforting sense of tradition for the public and also enhance the cultural value of the built environment."[20] Thus, more than 175 years after classicism first arrived in Mobile, its pleasing rhythms still appeal to architects, builders, and residents alike.

Mobile today is very much a modern American port city with all of the things one would expect of such a place — a container port, a cruise ship, skyscrapers, airports, interstate highways, malls, hospitals, schools, athletic and artistic enterprises. But more importantly, Mobile is an old and house-proud town, boasting thousands of historic buildings on tree-canopied streets. Central to its historic ambience are the Greek Revival buildings erected so long ago. Truly, a profound debt of gratitude is owed to Roper, Hitchcock, Gallier, the Dakins, Palmer, Collins, James, Barnes, Bunnell, Butt, and all the rest who labored, suffered, and bequeathed so distinguished and lovely a legacy.

ABBREVIATIONS

BA Barton Academy

CEP Christ Episcopal Church

GSPC Government Street Presbyterian Church

HMPS Historic Mobile Preservation Society

MA Municipal Archives, City of Mobile

MAM Marian Acker MacPherson

MCHS Marengo County Historical Society

MHDC Mobile Historic Development Commission

MPL Mobile Public Library, Local History and Genealogy Division

NR National Register

PC Probate Court, Mobile County

WSHL W. S. Hoole Library, Tuscaloosa, Ala.

NOTES

PREFACE: *My Georgia Cottage*

1. A variety of sources approximate Georgia Cottage's construction date. "Minute Book" 1, 543, PC details how Mary J. Delbarco obtained title to the land in 1837. Deed Book 2, O.S. (Old Series), 432, PC describes William A. Hardaway and Mary J. Hardaway as "recently joined in marriage" in 1841. Deed Book 9, O.S., 698, PC records the transfer of the property "with all the improvements thereon" by the Hardaways to a trustee in 1855. City directories narrow the possibilities. The *City of Mobile Directory*, 1844, lists the Hardaways as living at the northeast corner of Church and Joachim streets, whereas the *City of Mobile Directory*, 1850–51, the next closest available year, lists their residence as in the "country." Therefore, a circa 1845 date best approximates the construction. For the Hardaways' ownership of slaves, Tax Records, 1843, Mobile County, Ala., MA.

2. On Augusta Jane Evans see Owen, *History of Alabama and Dictionary of Alabama Biography, 1782–83*. On the sale, see Deed Book 11, O.S., 451, PC. The price was $5,000. The quote is from Sexton, "The Letters of Augusta Evans Wilson," 62. Georgia Cottage has certainly proved to be an effective literary incubator. In addition to Augusta Evans Wilson's labors, there are my father's famous World War II memoirs, *With the Old Breed* (1981) and *China Marine* (2002), as well as my own modest histories.

3. On the Sledges' acquisition, Deed Book 257, 294, PC. See also the *Mobile Register*, October 20, 1935. Of Gran's many tales, one remains vivid. When I was very young and fascinated by the Alamo, she showed me what she claimed was a brass powder flask from the siege. I excitedly shared this with my father, who guffawed and hooted, "Hell, that's a GI oilcan like I used in the Pacific!"

4. The Charles Lamb story is almost certainly apocryphal; either imagined by Gran or fed her by an overzealous Crescent City antiques dealer. The latter may, in fact, have been the case, because the Bellingrath Home southwest of Mobile also has a piece of Empire furniture acquired in New Orleans that reportedly belonged to Lamb. But because he died in 1834, and had no children, the reality is that these 1850s pieces probably belonged to a lateral descendent in Louisiana. My thanks to Tom McGehee, curator at the Bellingrath Home, for pointing this out to me.

INTRODUCTION:
Greek Revival Architecture in America

1. Hill, Stevens, and Burkett, *The Hill Readers*, 224.
2. Pierson, *American Buildings*, 61–65.
3. Ibid., 206, 207.
4. Wiebenson, *Sources of Greek Revival Architecture*, 18, 26. Volume 1 of Stuart and Revett was published in 1762, volume 2 in 1789, volume 3 in 1794, and volume 4 in 1816. A fifth supplemental volume, much less important than the original four, was published in 1830.
5. Lawrence, "Stuart and Revett," 128.
6. Kennedy, *Greek Revival America*, 344.
7. On these buildings see Hamlin, *Greek Revival Architecture in America*, 559 (the Admiralty), 506 (Brandenburg Gate), and 558 (British Museum).
8. For a thorough discussion of these buildings, see

Pierson, *American Buildings*, 292–93 (Monticello), 293–98 (Virginia capitol), and 326–32 (University of Virginia).

9. Quote is from Hamlin, *Greek Revival Architecture in America*, 36. On the Bank of Pennsylvania, see Maynard, *Architecture in the United States*, 223–25.
10. McNeal, *Nicholas Biddle in Greece*, 49.
11. Ibid., 50.
12. "Girard College and Its Founder," *North American Review*, 95.
13. On Philadelphia's importance, see Hamlin, *Greek Revival Architecture in America*, 63, 67.
14. On the Fairmount Waterworks and Graff, see Maynard, *Architecture in the United States*, 40–41.
15. Pierson, *American Buildings*, 436.
16. On construction materials, see Maynard, *Architecture in the United States*, 227–29.
17. On these buildings see Maynard, *Architecture in the United States*, 230 (Merchants' Exchange), 231–33 (Girard College), and 241 (Andalusia).
18. Trollope, *Domestic Manners of the Americans*, 79 (the banks), and 74 (the Waterworks).
19. Dickens, *American Notes for General Circulation*, 43.
20. Buckingham, *America, Historical, Statistic, and Descriptive*, 334 (the Second Bank), 339–40 (Girard College), and 340 (Waterworks).
21. "The American Builder's General Price Book and Estimator," *North American Review*, 360.
22. Hone, *Diary of Philip Hone*, 289.
23. Shippee, *Bishop Whipple's Southern Diary*, 173.
24. Oldmixon, *Transatlantic Wanderings*, 42–43.
25. Gallier, *Autobiography of James Gallier*, 9.
26. Ibid., 18.
27. Ibid. American architecture became more formally professional in 1836, when Strickland, Walter, and James Dakin founded the American Institution of Architects. Twenty years later this evolved into the American Institute of Architects (AIA), which still promotes and regulates the profession. See Hamlin, *Greek Revival Architecture in America*, 60.
28. Benjamin, *Architect*, vii.
29. Ibid., v.
30. Lafever, *Beauties*, 1.
31. Ibid., plate 32. There are no page numbers for the plates or their accompanying descriptions.
32. Nicholson, *The Mechanic's Companion*, 324–25.
33. Gallier, *Autobiography of James Gallier*, 33.
34. Rosenstiel and Winkler, *Floor Coverings*, 120.
35. Trollope, *Domestic Manners of the Americans*, 191. Nineteenth-century Americans often referred to Empire furniture as "Grecian."
36. Trollope, *Domestic Manners of the Americans*, 192.
37. "Some Observations," *Manufacturer and Builder*, 62–63.
38. On Town and Davis, see Scully, *James Dakin, Architect*, 4.
39. For a full discussion of these innovations, see Scully, *James Dakin, Architect*, 5, 6.
40. Gallier, *Autobiography of James Gallier*, 19.
41. Scully, *James Dakin, Architect*, 39, 40.
42. Turner and Meek, *Gardens of Louisiana*, 7.
43. *DeBow's Review*, August 1861, 189.
44. On these buildings, see Gamble, *The Alabama Catalog*, 52 (the Capitol), 54 (Forks of Cypress), and 53 (Spring Hill College).
45. *Alabama Intelligencer and State's Rights Expositor*, April 20, 1831.
46. Magnolia Hall Contract, W. S. Hoole Library. The Ionic capitals on Magnolia Hall are cast iron.
47. On these buildings, see Gamble, *The Alabama Catalog*, 323–24 (Capitol), 275 (Gaineswood), and 223 (Sturdivant Hall).

48. Abbott, *South and North*, 119.
49. Kennedy, *Greek Revival America*, 189.
50. Hamlin, *Greek Revival Architecture in America*, 62.
51. Cooper, *Home As Found*, 128.
52. "Architecture," *New Englander and Yale Review*, August 1850, 421.
53. "Our Houses," *Harper's*, September 1859, 514.
54. Van Rensselaer, "Recent Architecture in America," 49.
55. Gamble, "The White-Column Tradition," 55.
56. Wilson and Ferris, *Encyclopedia of Southern Culture*, 1137.
57. Faulkner, *Sartoris*, 7. *Sartoris* was republished in an expanded version as *Flags in the Dust* in 1973.
58. Harwell, *Margaret Mitchell's Gone with the Wind Letters*, 255.
59. On advertising, see Kirby, *Media-Made Dixie*, 74–75. On the Natchez pilgrimage see www.natchezpilgrimage.com.
60. Frank, "Ghosts and Ruins."
61. Hamlin, *Greek Revival Architecture in America*, 4. Hamlin's thesis has gained an amazing degree of traction over the decades and is still routinely accepted and repeated by popular architectural magazines and books as well as by homes tour guides all across America.
62. Maynard, *Architecture in the United States*, 249.
63. Gowans, *Images of American Living*, 281.
64. Gamble, "The White-Column Tradition," 55, 51.
65. Lobell, "Doric, Ironic, and Labyrinthian."
66. On the universities, see Falatko, "Classical Education," 117. For the institute's mission statement see www.classicist.org/about. On the Habitat for Humanity partnership see www.habitat.org/newsroom/2005archive/insitedoc0o8o80.aspx and Colman, "Mid 18th-century Modern."
67. Bierman, "Fit to Print."

CHAPTER ONE.
Pillared Beginnings in Antebellum Mobile

1. *Memorial of The Mayor and Aldermen*, 4.
2. All quotes are from the *Mobile Commercial Register*, February 17, 1822.
3. On Judson and Hobart, see Gould, *From Fort to Port*, 45, and *From Builders to Architects*, 13–15.
4. Will Book, 1:143, PC.
5. *Mobile Commercial Register*, July 23, 1828.
6. Misc. Book B, 42–44, PC. For a full analysis of the first courthouse, see Gould, *From Builders to Architects*, 17–19.
7. *Mobile Commercial Register*, October 27, 1827.
8. Ibid.
9. Thomas Hamilton, *Men and Manners in America*, 361
10. On Portier and Spring Hill College, see Thomason, *Mobile*, 69, and Gould, *From Fort to Port*, 101–2.
11. On Beroujon, see Gould, *From Fort to Port*, 88. For a description of the building, see p. 102.
12. Quote is from Gamble, *The Alabama Catalog*, 53.
13. On the first American hospital, see Gould, *From Fort to Port*, 58.
14. Aldermen's Minutes, April 17, 1833, 90. MA.
15. Ibid., August 28, 1833, 117.
16. The *City of Mobile Directory*, 1837, is the earliest available. On the fee, see Gould, *From Fort to Port*, 60.
17. On Collins as Hobart's executor, see Will Book 1:142, PC. On his fee for the hospital, see Gould, *From Fort to Port*, 60. The quotation is from "Interesting Transcriptions from the City Documents," 1823–44, 112.
18. "Notes on the Old City Hospital Building," Lucy Nelson, n.d., file, 850 St. Anthony Street, MHDC.
19. On Roper, see Schumann, "'Cook's House' Exhibit," 2–3.

20. On the death of Roper's wife, see *Oakleigh Period House Museum*, 8. On the name Oakleigh, see Schumann, "'Cook's House' Exhibit," 2.
21. File, 350 Oakleigh Place, MHDC. This file contains a complete chain of title and tax information taken from primary sources.
22. Schumann, "'Cook's House' Exhibit," 2–3.
23. On cotton exports, see Amos, *Cotton City*, 21.
24. On cotton prices, see Jordan, "Antebellum Mobile," 190.
25. On imports, see Amos, *Cotton City*, 23.
26. Jordan, "Antebellum Mobile," 189.
27. "Interesting Transcriptions from the City Documents," 1820–1911, 455.
28. *Independent Chronicle and Boston Patriot*, November 11, 1835.
29. Lane, *Architecture of the Old South*, 52.
30. Jordan, "Antebellum Mobile," 192.
31. Scully, *James Dakin, Architect*, 40.
32. Gallier, *Autobiography of James Gallier*, 21.
33. Scully, *James Dakin, Architect*, 40–41.
34. Ibid., 68.
35. Gallier, *Autobiography of James Gallier*, 21.
36. On Hitchcock's career, see Beidler, "Toulmin and Hitchcock," 22–23, and Owen, *History of Alabama*, 3:816. Hitchcock's wife signed her name "Ann."
37. Brantley, "Henry Hitchcock," 21, 22.
38. *Mobile Commercial Register*, February 7, 1822.
39. Amos, *Cotton City*, 81.
40. Ibid., 80.
41. *Mobile Commercial Register*, November 25, 1835.
42. Rita K. Thompson, "Tradesmen Information." This spreadsheet of antebellum tradesmen and their birthplaces was compiled from census data and city directories.
43. On Mechanics House, see Rita K. Thompson, *Building Mobile, Alabama*, 25. On antebellum vice and amusements, see Amos, *Cotton City*, 148–50.
44. On the ordinance, see *Code of Ordinances*, 1859, 348–49, which lists the earlier year that this law originally passed.
45. On the Society, see Amos, *Cotton City*, 97. On militia and fire companies, and other social outlets, see ibid., 63–64.
46. Mannhard, "Free People of Color," 16, for the number of free blacks in Mobile. Occupations are listed on p. 75, and the individuals are listed on p. 77.
47. The quote is from Lane, *Architecture of the Old South*, 59. See also *City of Mobile Directory*, 1837.
48. See *City of Mobile Directories*, 1837–52.
49. On James, see Craighead, "Dropped Stitches from Mobile's Past," *Mobile Register*, February 2, 1929.
50. *City of Mobile Directories*, 1838–52.
51. *Eighth Census*, Mobile Co., Ala. MPL.
52. *Tharin's Marengo County Directory for 1860–61*.
53. *City of Mobile Directory*, 1859.
54. Misc. Book C, 48, PC.
55. Invoice, box 18001, envelope 3, folder 3, MA.
56. On hiring out slaves, see Amos, *Cotton City*, 88–89.
57. Waselkov and Gums, *Plantation Archaeology*, 203.
58. "Interesting Transcriptions from the City Documents," 1845–67, 55.
59. See Eisterhold, "Mobile: Lumber Center of the Gulf Coast," 85–86 (Hobart's mill), 89–90 (Deshon's mill), and 95–97 (lumberyards in town).
60. *Collection of the Ordinances*, 1835, 57.
61. See *City of Mobile Directory*, 1839.
62. On Mobile when Dakin arrived, see *Mobile Commercial Register*, December 31, 1835, and Scully, *James Dakin, Architect*, 68. On his ownership of Lafever's book, see Scully, 71.

CHAPTER TWO.
Pillared City, Pillared Ruin, 1836–1839

1. On the partnership, see Scully, *James Dakin, Architect*, 51, 68. See also *City of Mobile Directory*, 1837, which shows the office at a new location on the south side of Government Street, near Royal.
2. Gallier, *Autobiography of James Gallier*, 21.
3. Rev. William T. Hamilton, *Funeral Discourse*, 7–8.
4. On Mobile's early Presbyterians, see Bates, *Archives Tell a Story*, 25, and Sledge, "Ornament to the City," 37–38.
5. On the land acquisition, see Deed Book P, 663, PC. The ad is in the *Mobile Commercial Register*, December 17, 1835.
6. Scully, *James Dakin, Architect*, 71. On Gallier importing materials to New Orleans, see Gallier, *Autobiography of James Gallier*, 22.
7. Session Minutes, March 22, 1837, 204, GSPC. James Roper was remarried here in November 1838.
8. Session Minutes, March 24, 1837, 182.
9. *Mobile Commercial Register*, June 1, 1837.
10. Sledge and Gamble, GSPC NHL nomination form, 6. The church was listed as an NHL in 1994. Mobile's other NHL is the Southern Market/City Hall, an Italianate building that presently serves as the Museum of Mobile.
11. For a full description see Sledge and Gamble, GSPC NHL nomination form, 4–5.
12. Scully, *James Dakin, Architect*, 71. See also Gould, *From Fort to Port*, 66–67.
13. Watson, *History of Barton Academy*, 12.
14. On funding sources, see Amos, *Cotton City*, 180–81. On the site acquisition, see Deed Book I:213, PC.
15. *Mobile Commercial Register*, December 6, 1835.
16. School Board Minutes, November 9, 1836, 10, BA.
17. On the various contractors, see ibid., February 18, 1837, 18.
18. School Board Minutes, October 5, 1836, 9, BA.
19. Ibid., March 9, 1837, 21.
20. Ibid., April 12, 1837, 23.
21. Ibid., August 2, 1837, 26 (meetings); September 2, 1837, 32 (interior painted); January 2, 1839, 44 (shade trees planted).
22. On Barton's early use, see Amos, *Cotton City*, 182. Barton became a public school in 1852.
23. Scully, *James Dakin, Architect*, 75–76.
24. *Seventh Census*, Mobile Co., Ala., MPL. See also the 1839 tax records, MA.
25. Amos, *Cotton City*, 50.
26. *Mobile Commercial Register*, November 7, 1836.
27. Gallier, *Autobiography of James Gallier*, 27.
28. Scully, *James Dakin, Architect*, 76–77.
29. Lane, *Architecture of the Old South*, 59–61.
30. Lipscomb, *Mobile's Cathedral, 1850–2004*, 18.
31. Sledge, "Thematic Group Creole and Gulf Coast Cottages," 7. Creole cottages are found all along the central Gulf Coast, as well as in the Mississippi Valley. Pensacola, Fla.; Mobile; Biloxi, Miss.; New Orleans, La.; and St. Genevieve, Mo., all have impressive examples.
32. File, Portier House, 307 Conti Street, MHDC. The quote is from a report to Monsignor Fransoni, Prefect of the Propaganda, Rome, cited in the file.
33. File, Hall-Ford House, 165 St. Emanuel Street, MHDC.
34. Brantley, "Henry Hitchcock of Mobile," 16.
35. On the Panic of 1837, see Brantley, "Henry Hitchcock of Mobile," 24–25. Baldwin's quote is from *Flush Times of Alabama and Mississippi*, p. 90.
36. Schumann, "'Cook's House' Exhibit," 3. The brother-in-law was only able to purchase about half the original acreage with the house.
37. Alan Smith Thompson, "Mobile, Alabama,

1850–1861," 74 (real estate figures), 75 (bank closures), and 76 (municipal default).
38. *Niles Weekly Register.*
39. Misc. Book C, 103, PC.
40. Scully, *James Dakin, Architect*, 82.
41. Lipscomb, *Mobile's Cathedral, 1850-2004*, 22.
42. Rev. William T. Hamilton, *Funeral Discourse*, 10.
43. Hitchcock papers, box 641, folder 13, Ann Hitchcock letter, April 16, 1837, WSHL.
44. Hitchcock papers, box 641, folder 14, May 5, 1837, WSHL.
45. Ibid., November 6, 1838.
46. Ibid., box 641, folder 18, November 6, 1838.
47. Brantley, "Henry Hitchcock of Mobile," 30–33.
48. *Mobile Commercial Register.*
49. Gould, *From Fort to Port*, 68–69.
50. Christ Church Records, 1828–54, 22–23, CEP.
51. On Christ Church as a New York building, see Scully, *James Dakin, Architect*, 80. On the contract, see Misc. Book C, 166–73, PC.
52. Christ Church Records, 1828–54, 58.
53. Misc. Book C, 166–73, PC.
54. *Mobile Commercial Register.* See also File, 114 St. Emanuel Street, Christ Episcopal Church, MHDC.
55. On the population, see Amos, *Cotton City*, 86.
56. "Interesting Transcriptions," 1815–59, 76, MA.
57. *Mobile Commercial Register*, February 16, 1839.
58. Buckingham, *Slave States of America*, 1:282–83. Buckingham left Mobile to tour other cities, including Philadelphia, where he arrived in 1840.
59. Buckingham, *Slave States of America*, 1:287.
60. On the epidemic's severity, see *Mobile Commercial Register*, November 4, 1839, which lists deaths per month — 139 in August, 360 in September, and 120 in October. The quote is from the Hamilton papers, Sermon, November 26, 1863, GSPC.
61. Rev. William T. Hamilton, *Funeral Discourse*, 16–17. Five other Mobilians died that day — three children and two slaves — and twenty-six people were dead by week's end. See *Mobile Commercial Register*, August 12, 1839.
62. *Mobile Commercial Register*, August 13, 1839.
63. Ibid., August 14, 1839. Hitchcock's plot in Magnolia Cemetery includes his obelisk surrounded by a cast iron fence with anthemion crests and a pair of lyres in the gate — all appropriately Greek Revival for the man who did so much to introduce the style to Mobile. Among the stone's inscriptions is Psalm 37:37 —"Mark the perfect man, and behold the upright: for the end of that man is peace."
64. In recognition of Hitchcock's reputation for architectural excellence, the Mobile Historic Development Commission gives the Henry Hitchcock Award to a worthy historic building each year. The criteria stipulate that the building must be at least a century old and "possess exceptional value or quality in illustrating or interpreting the heritage of Mobile in history, architecture, archeology, technology and culture; and possess a high degree of integrity of location, design, setting, materials, workmanship, feeling, and association." The award is a handsome wreathed iron plaque that is bolted onto the wall.
65. On protective measures, see Gould, *From Fort to Port*, 77. The quote is from "Interesting Transcriptions," 1820–1911, 473, MA.
66. On the fires, see *Mobile Mercantile Advertiser*, October 8, 1839. Quote from Goodman to Dellet, October 8, 1839. James Dellet papers, collection of Charles Torrey.
67. *Mobile Mercantile Advertiser*, October 9, 1839.
68. On the fire, see *New Orleans Daily Picayune*, October 11, 1839. On the firemen and for the cistern quote, see Delaney, *Craighead's Mobile*,

84. On Hamilton, see John Gaillard Hamilton, "Hamilton Genealogy," 5.
69. Delaney, *Craighead's Mobile*, 83–84.
70. *Pennsylvanian*, October 22, 1839.
71. *Philadelphia Courier*, October 28, 1839.
72. *Mobile Commercial Register*, October 18, 1839.
73. *Mobile Register and Journal*, June 1, 1843.
74. Pitts, *Life and Confession*, 38–41.
75. *Mobile Merchants and Planters Journal*, November 12, 1839.
76. Ibid.

CHAPTER THREE.
Town and Country Classicism, 1840–1865

1. On Mobile's designation as the "Paris of the Confederacy," see O'Brien, *Mobile, 1865*, 17.
2. The notice is from *Mobile Commercial Register*, February 15, 1840. The newspaper reversed the bank's name. On speculation as to who the "Architect" was, see Scully, *James Dakin, Architect*, 82. The new bank would be torn down in the 1930s. James Dakin continued to practice architecture successfully in New Orleans and Baton Rouge until his death in 1852.
3. *New Orleans Daily Picayune*, November 30, 1839.
4. Amos, *Cotton City*, 124.
5. "Interesting Transcriptions," 1820–1911, 485.
6. Meriwether, "A Southern Traveler's Diary," 136–37.
7. Koch, *Journey*, 109.
8. Shippee, *Bishop Whipple's Southern Diary*, 86–87.
9. Ibid., 88.
10. Ibid., 92.
11. Ibid., 88–89 (slave auction), 91 (markets), 92–93 (Henry Clay).
12. On 1840s construction, see Gould, *From Fort to Port*, 105.
13. File, Marine Hospital, 800 St. Anthony Street, MHDC. See especially the National Register nomination documentation in the file. On the bids, see *Mobile Commercial Register*, April 4, 1839.
14. File, Marine Hospital, MHDC.
15. File, Waring Texas, 110 S. Claiborne Street, MHDC.
16. There is no listing for John Nugent in either the 1840 or the 1850 census records. This is unfortunate, since these records usually include the birthplace of those enumerated.
17. File, Conde-Charlotte House, 104 St. Emanuel Street, MHDC.
18. Ibid.
19. On the farm acquisition, see Deed Book 5, O.S., 147, PC. On Carlen family see File, 54 S. Carlen Street, MHDC.
20. On the Dawson House, see Gould, *From Fort to Port*, 121–23. On the fifteen house slaves, see Hammond, *Antebellum Mansions of Alabama*, 169. See also *Seventh Census, Slave Schedule*, Mobile County, Ala., MPL. The children were a one-year-old girl and two boys, aged four and six.
21. Amos, *Cotton City*, see charts on pp. 21, 23.
22. Amos, *Cotton City*, 96.
23. Seale, "Bragg-Mitchell Report," 14.
24. Lipscomb, *Mobile's Cathedral*, 29.
25. *Mobile Daily Register*, May 6, 1852.
26. Ibid., March 2, 1853.
27. The contract is in Misc. Book F, 71–72, PC. For a good description of the building, see Gould, *From Fort to Port*, 132.
28. Olmstead, *Cotton Kingdom*, 282.
29. Seale, "Bragg-Mitchell Report," 15.
30. Bremer, *Homes of the New World*, 2:217.
31. Oldmixon, *Transatlantic Wanderings*, 155.
32. Ibid., 154.
33. *City of Mobile Directory*, 1859.
34. Amos, *Cotton City*, 92 (table listing occupa-

tions) and 82 (table listing employment in manufacturing).
35. *City of Mobile Directory*, 1859.
36. *Mobile Daily Register*, March 13, 1850.
37. Smith, *White Pillars*, 93.
38. Gould, Number 5 Fire Station, NR nomination. On the uniforms and engine name, see File, 7 North Lawrence Street, MHDC.
39. File, 910 Government Street, MHDC. See also Gould, *From Fort to Port*, 154–55.
40. File, 307 North Conception Street, MHDC.
41. File, 401 Church Street, MHDC.
42. File, 1614 Old Shell Road, MHDC.
43. *Alabama Planter*, April 17, 1854. James Garfield visited Oakleigh in 1877, but that was before he was elected president.
44. File, Stewartfield, MHDC.
45. John Gaillard Hamilton, "Hamilton Genealogy," 33–34.
46. Gould, *From Fort to Port*, 150.
47. File, 152 Tuthill Lane, MHDC. See also *Mobile Press-Register*, March 20, 1966.
48. Alabama Historical Commission, *Alabama Ante-Bellum Architecture*, 76.
49. Seale, "Bragg-Mitchell Report," 16.
50. Ibid., 41. Thomas James is mentioned in Hammond, *Antebellum Mansions of Alabama*, 167. Gamble, *The Alabama Catalog*, 78, attributes the design to Alexander J. Bragg, who did work in the Black Belt.
51. Seale, "Bragg-Mitchell Report," 45.
52. Hammond, *Antebellum Mansions of Alabama*, 168.
53. File, 607 Government Street, MHDC.
54. Peter Joseph Hamilton, *Little Boy*, 7–8.
55. Ibid.
56. Amos, *Cotton City*, 238 on secessionist sentiment. See Seale, "Bragg-Mitchell Report," 18–19, and File, 152 Tuthill Lane, MHDC, for Bragg and Marshall's wartime activities.
57. Bates, *Archives Tell a Story*, 85.
58. Watson, *History of Barton Academy*, 32.
59. *Mobile Register*, February 2, 1929.
60. Stone, *Wandering to Glory*, 121. *Beulah* was published in 1859.
61. Riepma, *Fire and Fiction*, 100.
62. *Mobile Commercial Register*, January 31, 1864. Another courthouse was not built until 1874. Several interim courthouses were utilized during this ten-year period, an indication of Reconstruction poverty.
63. *Mobile Commercial Register*, February 11, 1864.
64. Wallace, "Diary," 22.
65. Bergeron, *Confederate Mobile*, 93.
66. *Mobile Press-Register*, April 30, 1967. Moore's observations are summarized in the article. Though the diary is cited, I could not turn up a copy.
67. Peter Joseph Hamilton, *Little Boy*, 29–30.
68. Fonde, *Account of the Great Explosion*, 7. The explosion was audible in Fort Morgan, thirty-five miles south, and passengers aboard a train forty miles north of the city heard it above the locomotive noise.
69. *Mobile Press-Register*, April 30, 1967. The exact number of dead was never determined. Most estimates then and now range between two and five hundred. On hospital admissions, see Bailey, "Mobile's Tragedy," 47.
70. *Mobile Press-Register*, April 30, 1967.
71. McLaurin and Thomason, *Mobile*, 69.
72. Lipscomb, *Mobile's Cathedral, 1850–2004*, 40.

EPILOGUE: *The Long Reverberation*
1. *Mobile Weekly Register*, February 13, 1869.
2. *Mobile Press-Register*, February 2, 1969. The article reprinted original accounts of the fire on the centennial.
3. Acker, *Etchings of Old Mobile*, 82.
4. Beck, *Ghosts of Old Mobile*, 47.

5. Sledge Family Papers.
6. Thomason, *Mobile*, 190.
7. *Oakleigh Period House Museum* brochure. File, 350 Oakleigh Place, MHDC. I am indebted to Peggy Denniston for information about her family's tenure at the property.
8. Seale, "Bragg-Mitchell Report," 32, 38.
9. Ibid., 40–41.
10. See www.braggmitchellmansion.com.
11. File, Kirkbride House, MHDC.
12. File, 850 St. Anthony Street, MHDC.
13. Ibid.
14. *Mobile Register*, October 22, 1936.
15. Ibid., March 29, 1963.
16. Ibid.
17. *Mobile Press*, March 3, 1969.
18. Gregory and Mertins, "Places in Peril," 32. See also Daugherty, " Disgrace of Barton," 80.
19. On recent restoration efforts, see File, 504 Government Street, MHDC.
20. E-mail communication to author, April 27, 2007.

GLOSSARY

Grateful acknowledgement is made to Robert S. Gamble and the University of Alabama Press for permission to adapt some of the following definitions from *The Alabama Catalog, Historic American Buildings Survey: A Guide to the Early Architecture of the State*, copyright 1987 by The University of Alabama Press, all rights reserved.

abacus. The topmost portion of a column capital, on which the entablature rests, especially the square topmost member of a Doric capital.

acanthus. A neoclassical motif based on the leaf of a common Mediterranean plant.

antefixae. A decorative, upright ornament, most commonly a palmette or anthemion, used in a series along the ridge of a roof or atop the cornice of an entablature.

anthemion. A classical detail based on the palm leaf.

architrave. 1) The lowest part of the classical entablature, which rests directly on the column or pier capitals, with the frieze and cornice above. 2) The trim around a door or window.

arris. The raised edge between the flutings of a Doric column.

ashlar. Squared stonework. Often imitated in stucco by scoring.

capital. The top of a column or pilaster, rendered in one of the five orders.

cast iron. Iron that is poured into a mold.

Choragic Monument of Lysicrates. A famous classical monument (also called Demosthenes' lantern), distinguished by a circular peristyle with a low peaked roof. This form was much used in antebellum America for cupolas and gazebos.

Composite order. The last of the five classic orders, a Roman elaboration of the Corinthian order combining the acanthus leaf motif of the Corinthian capital with the volutes of the Ionic order, among other embellishments.

Corinthian order. The most elaborate of the three original classical orders. The fluted, narrow shaft is capped by a florid capital decorated with acanthus leaves and other elements.

cornice. In Greek Revival architecture, the topmost or projecting part of the entablature, with the frieze below.

cresting. An ornamental finish along a roof ridge or at the top of a wall.

denticulation. A decorative row of dentils, or small blocks, forming part of a classical entablature.

distyle in antis. A portico with two columns set between the piers or flanking end walls.

Doric order. The oldest and simplest of the original three classical orders. No base, fluted shaft, rounded capital.

eared architrave. A door or window architrave with tabs, or ears, at the upper corners.

egg and dart. A classical decorative motif composed of alternating egg-shaped and dart-shaped elements.

entablature. In classical architecture, the ornamental horizontal beam carried by the columns, divided into three parts: architrave (bottom), the frieze (middle), and the cornice (top).

entasis. The slight outward bulge of the shaft of a column; used to correct the optical illusion of concavity that would result from a straight-sided column.

Erechtheum. Classical temple in the Ionic order

situated on the Acropolis. Dedicated to Athena and famous for its Porch of Maidens, supported by the Carytids.

fanlight. A semicircular window, with radiating muntins, or tracery, set over a door. A popular motif of the Federal style.

fluted. Having regularly spaced, parallel grooves (flutes), as on the shaft of a column or pilaster.

frieze. An ornamental band that runs just below an eave line or cornice.

gable roof. A roof with two pitched slopes. The gable is the triangular segment beneath the slopes.

Gothic Revival. A popular architectural style during the middle to late nineteenth century. Distinguished by board and batten siding, steep roof pitch, lancet windows.

guttae. The row of peglike ornaments occurring on the mutules of a Doric frieze.

hexastyle. A row of six columns.

hip roof. A roof with four uniformly pitched sides.

in antis. A recessed portico with a row of columns between the antae, as in some Greek temples.

Ionic Order. One of the classic orders used in Greek and Roman architecture and its derivatives, characterized by its scroll-like capitals (volutes).

Italianate. Architectural style that flourished 1850–80. Influenced by the buildings and decorative arts of the Italian Renaissance. Distinguished by bracketed cornices, low hip roofs, rounded windows, and in Mobile, cast iron verandahs with floral motifs.

metope. The panel between the triglyphs in a Doric frieze.

mortise and tenon. An early form of frame construction in which heavy timbers were fitted together by means of mortises (holes or grooves) cut into one member to receive the tenons (corresponding projecting pieces) of another, the resulting joint secured by wooden pegs driven through both members. Superseded by balloon frame construction in the mid-nineteenth century.

mutule. One of the sloping flat blocks on the soffit of a Doric cornice, usually decorated with guttae.

order. A column together with its base and entablature, especially one of the five standard orders of classic architecture. The Greeks used three orders — Doric, Ionic, Corinthian — from which the Romans evolved derivatives, besides adding the Tuscan and Composite orders.

Parthenon. Centerpiece of the Acropolis, this classical Doric peripteral temple to Athena inspired nineteenth-century European and American architects of the Greek Revival.

pediment. The triangular face of a roof gable. Also, any similar triangular crowning element used over doors, windows, etc.

Pentelique. French word denoting marble quarried from Mount Penteli, near Athens. This was the source of marble used in many classical landmarks, including the Parthenon. Noted for its whiteness, softened by a touch of yellow, which makes it glow in sunlight.

peripteral. A colonnade that surrounds a building on all four sides.

pilaster. A shallow, flattened rectangular upright, applied to a wall and treated like a column, with base, shaft, and capital.

pilastrade. A row of pilasters.

plinth. The pedestal-like square or rectangular support on which a column rests.

portico. A formal porch attached to a building, usually supported by columns.

prostyle. A temple-type structure with columns across the front only.

quoin. One of the units of stone or brick accentuating the corners, angles, or openings of a wall. Can sometimes be simulated in raised stucco or plaster.

Second Empire. Architectural style popular during the latter half of the nineteenth century and inspired by French architecture under Napoleon III. Characterized by mansard roofs and heavy eaves.

segmental arch. Any rounded arch of less than a semicircle, thus a segment of a semicircular arch.

shaft. The main part of a column, between the base and the capital.

shutter dog. Hardware affixed to an exterior wall and designed to hold a shutter open. Frequently decorative, sometimes S-shaped.

stylobate. A continuous base or plinth on which a row of columns is set.

Temple of Theseus. Classical hexastyle Doric temple in the Athenian agora, dedicated to Athena and Hephaestus.

tetrastyle. A row of four columns.

Tower of the Winds. Famous Athenian monument erected in the second century BC as a weather vane and water clock. Its modified exterior Corinthian columns were illustrated in Minard Lafever's pattern book and were popular for antebellum interiors.

Town truss. A type of covered-bridge truss consisting of a latticelike network of overlapping triangles, so-called because it was patented by Ithiel Town in 1820. Much used in Alabama because it was so easy to erect.

triglyph. Characteristic of Doric-order frieze, consisting of a slightly raised block with V-shaped grooves. Triglyphs alternate with plain or sculptured panels called metopes.

Tuscan order. One of the classic orders used in Roman architecture, derived from the Doric but simpler, with a plain frieze and unfluted column shaft.

verandah. A covered porch or balcony.

volute. A spiral scroll-like motif such as that used, in pairs, as part of the Ionic capital. Also used with reference to the coil terminating a banister or handrail.

water table. The projecting base course of an exterior masonry wall, usually from the ground level to the first floor, which is beveled or molded at the top for weathering.

wrought iron. Iron that has been worked by a blacksmith with hammer and tong. Often used in fences in conjunction with cast iron.

BIBLIOGRAPHY

ARCHIVAL SOURCES
Aldermen's Minutes. MA.
Christ Church Records, 1828–54. CEP.
City of Mobile Directories, 1837–59. MA.
Code of Ordinances of the City of Mobile. Mobile: Goetzel & Co., 1859. MA.
Collection of the Ordinances Now in Force in the City of Mobile, 1835. Mobile: *Mercantile Advertiser*. MA.
Deed Books. PC.
Dellet, James, Papers. Charles Torrey private collection. Mobile.
Hamilton, John Gaillard. "Hamilton Genealogy." N.d. Palmer Hamilton Papers, Mobile.
Hamilton, Rev. William T., Papers. GSPC.
Historic buildings vertical files. MHDC.
Hitchcock, Henry, Papers. WSHL.
"Interesting Transcriptions from the City Documents of the City of Mobile." Vols. for 1815–59, 1820–1911, 1823–44, 1845–67. Prepared from original data by the Municipal and Court Records Project of the Works Progress Administration, 1939. MA.
Invoice records. MA.
Magnolia Hall Contract, ca. 1855. WSHL.
Minute Books. PC.
Miscellaneous Books. PC.
Nelson, Lucy. "Notes on the Old City Hospital Building." N.d. File, 850 St. Anthony Street. MHDC.
School Board Minutes. Vol. 1: 1836–45. BA.
Seale, William. "Bragg-Mitchell Report." 2000. MHDC.
Session Minutes. GSPC.
Sledge Family Papers. Author's collection.
Sledge, John S. "Thematic Group Creole and Gulf Coast Cottages in Baldwin County." National Register of Historic Places nomination form, 1987. MHDC.
Sledge, John S., and Robert Gamble. "Government Street Presbyterian Church." National Historic Landmark nomination form, 1992. MHDC.

Tax Records, Mobile County. MA.
Tharin's Marengo County Directory for 1860–61. MCHS.
Thompson, Rita K. "Tradesmen Information." Spreadsheet, 2008. MHDC.
U.S. Bureau of the Census. *Sixth Census of the United States, 1840. Population*. Mobile County, Ala. MPL.
———. *Seventh Census of the United States, 1850. Population*. Mobile County, Ala. MPL.
———. *Seventh Census of the United States, 1850. Slave Schedule*. Mobile County, Ala. MPL.
———. *Eighth Census of the United States, 1860. Population*. Mobile County, Ala. MPL.
Will Books. PC.

INTERVIEWS AND PERSONAL COMMUNICATIONS
Kearley, Douglas Burtu. E-mail to author, Mobile, Ala., April 27, 2007.

NEWSPAPERS
Alabama Intelligencer and State's Rights Expositor, 1831.
Alabama Planter, 1854.
Independent Chronicle and Boston Patriot, 1835.
Mobile Commercial Register, 1822–64.
Mobile Daily Register, 1850–52.
Mobile Mercantile Advertiser, 1839.
Mobile Merchants and Planters Journal, 1839.
Mobile Press, 1969.
Mobile Press-Register, 1966–69.
Mobile Register, 1929–63.
Mobile Register and Journal, 1843.
Mobile Weekly Register, 1869.
New Orleans Daily Picayune, 1839.
Niles Weekly Register, 1837.
Pennsylvanian, 1839.
Philadelphia Courier, 1839.

BOOKS, ARTICLES, AND OTHER SOURCES

Abbot, John S. C. *South and North.* New York: Abbey and Abbot, 1860.

Acker, Marian Francis. *Etchings of Old Mobile.* 1938. Reprint, Mobile: Marian Francis Acker, 1943.

Alabama Historical Commission. *Alabama Ante-Bellum Architecture: A Scrapbook View from the 1930s.* Auburn: University Printing Service, 1976.

"The American Builder's General Price Book and Estimator." *North American Review* 43, no. 93 (October 1836): 356–84.

Amos, Harriet. *Cotton City: Urban Development in Antebellum Mobile.* Tuscaloosa: University of Alabama Press, 1985.

"Architecture." *New Englander and Yale Review* 8, no. 31 (August 1850): 418–34.

Bailey, Mrs. Hugh C. "Mobile's Tragedy: The Great Magazine Explosion of 1865." *Alabama Review* 21, no. 1 (January 1968): 40–52.

Baldwin, Joseph G. *The Flush Times of Alabama and Mississippi: A Series of Sketches.* New York: D. Appleton, 1853.

Bates, Charles D. *The Archives Tell a Story of the Government Street Presbyterian Church.* Mobile: Gill Printing Co., 1959.

Beck, Mary Randelette. *Ghosts of Old Mobile.* Mobile: Haunted Book Shop, 1946.

Beidler, Phil. "Toulmin and Hitchcock, Pioneering Jurists of the Alabama Frontier." *Alabama Heritage* 81 (Summer 2006): 18–25.

Benjamin, Asher. *The Architect, or Practical House Carpenter.* 1830. Reprint, New York: Dover Publications Inc., 1988.

Bergeron, Arthur W. *Confederate Mobile.* Jackson: University Press of Mississippi, 1991.

Bierman, M. Lindsay. "Fit to Print." *Architecture,* November 1994, 76–77.

Brantley, William H. "Henry Hitchcock of Mobile, 1816–39." *Alabama Review* 5, no. 1 (January 1952): 3–39.

Bremer, Fredrika. *The Homes of the New World: Impressions of America.* 2 vols. New York: Harper & Brothers, 1854.

Buckingham, J. S. *America, Historical, Statistic, and Descriptive.* New York: Harper Brothers, 1841.

———. *Slave States of America.* 2 vols. London: Fisher, Son and Co., 1842.

Colman, David. "Mid 18th-century Modern: The Classicists Strike Back." *New York Times,* February 10, 2005.

Cooper, James Fenimore. *Home As Found.* 1838. Reprint, New York: Stringer and Townsend, 1852.

Craighead, Erwin. "Dropped Stitches from Mobile's Past." *Mobile Register,* February 2, 1929.

Daugherty, Franklin. "The Disgrace of Barton." *Mobile Bay Monthly* 21, no. 8 (August 2005): 80–83.

Delaney, Caldwell, ed. *Craighead's Mobile: Being the Fugitive Writings of Erwin S. Craighead and Frank Craighead.* Mobile: Haunted Book Shop, 1968.

DeBow's Review 31, no. 2 (August 1861): 189.

Dickens, Charles. *American Notes for General Circulation.* 1842. Reprint, New York: Appleton and Company, 1868.

Eisterhold, John A. "Mobile: Lumber Center of the Gulf Coast." *Alabama Review* 24, no. 2 (April 1973): 83–104.

Falatko, Stephen. "Classical Education." *Architecture,* November 1994, 117.

Faulkner, William. *Sartoris.* New York: Harcourt, Brace and Co., 1929.

Fonde, Charles H. *An Account of the Great Magazine Explosion of the United States Ordnance Stores Which Occurred in Mobile on the 25th Day of May 1865.* Mobile: Henry Farrow and Son, 1869.

Frank, Michael. "Ghosts and Ruins along the Mississippi." *New York Times,* September 20, 1998.

Gallier, James. *Autobiography of James Gallier.* Paris: E. Briere, 1864.

Gamble, Robert. *The Alabama Catalog, Historic American Buildings Survey: A Guide to the Early Architecture of the State.* Tuscaloosa: University of Alabama Press, 1987.

———. "The White-Column Tradition." *Southern Humanities Review*, Special Issue 1977, 41–59.

"Girard College and Its Founder." *North American Review* 100, no. 206 (January 1865): 70–101.

Gould, Elizabeth B. *From Builders to Architects: The Hobart-Hutchisson Six*. Montgomery: Black Belt Press, 1997.

———. *From Fort to Port: An Architectural History of Mobile, Alabama, 1711–1918*. Tuscaloosa: University of Alabama Press, 1988.

Gowans, Alan. *Images of American Living*. New York: Lippincott, 1964.

Gregory, Melanie Betz, and Ellen Mertins. "Places in Peril: Alabama's Endangered Historic Landmarks for 2005." *Alabama Heritage* 78 (Fall 2005): 30–39.

Hamilton, Peter Joseph. *A Little Boy in Confederate Mobile*. Mobile: Colonial Mobile Bookshop, 1947.

Hamilton, Rev. William T. *A Funeral Discourse in Memory of Judge Henry Hitchcock*. Mobile: *Advertiser and Chronicle*, 1839.

Hamilton, Thomas. *Men and Manners in America*. 1833. Reprint, Edinburgh: Blackwood and Sons, 1843.

Hamlin, Talbot. *Greek Revival Architecture in America*. Oxford: Oxford University Press, 1944.

Hammond, Ralph. *Antebellum Mansions of Alabama*. New York: Architectural Book Co., 1951.

Harwell, Richard, ed. *Margaret Mitchell's Gone with the Wind Letters, 1936–49*. New York: MacMillan, 1976.

Hill, Daniel Harvey, Frank Lincolns Stevens, and Charles William Burkett. *The Hill Readers*. Boston: Ginn and Company, 1906.

Hone, Philip. *The Diary of Philip Hone*. Vol. I, *1828–51*. New York: Dodd, Mead, 1869.

Jordan, Weymouth T. "Antebellum Mobile: Alabama's Agricultural Emporium." *Alabama Review* 1, no. 3 (July 1948): 180–202.

Kennedy, Roger. *Greek Revival America*. New York: Stewart, Tabori, and Chang, 1989.

Kirby, Jack Temple. *Media-Made Dixie*. Baton Rouge: Louisiana State University Press, 1978.

Koch, Albert C. *Journey Through a Part of North America in the Years 1844 to 1846*. Reprint, Carbondale: Southern Illinois University Press, 1972.

Lafever, Minard. *The Beauties of Modern Architecture*. New York: Appleton, 1835.

Lane, Mills. *Architecture of the Old South: Mississippi and Alabama*. Savannah: Beehive Press, 1997.

Lawrence, Lesley. "Stuart and Revett: Their Literary and Architectural Careers." *Journal of the Warburg Institute* 12, no. 2 (October 1938): 128–46.

Lipscomb, Oscar. *Mobile's Cathedral, 1850–2004*. Mobile: Archdiocese of Mobile, 2005.

Lobell, John. "Doric, Ironic, and Labyrinthian: Classical Architecture in America." *Skyline* 3, no. 2 (February 1980): 10.

Mannhard, Marilyn. "The Free People of Color in Antebellum Mobile County, Alabama." Thesis, University of South Alabama, 1982.

Maynard, W. Barksdale. *Architecture in the United States, 1800–1850*. New Haven: Yale University Press, 2002.

McLaurin, Melton, and Michael V. R. Thomason. *Mobile: The Life and Times of a Great Southern City*. Woodland Hills, Ca.: Windsor Publications, 1981.

McNeal, R. A., ed. *Nicholas Biddle in Greece: The Journals and Letters of 1806*. Philadelphia: Pennsylvania State University Press, 1993.

Memorial of the Mayor and Aldermen of the City of Mobile. Washington, D.C.: Gales and Seaton, 1820.

Meriwether, Colyer, ed. "'A Southern Traveler's Diary in 1840' by William H. Wills." *Publications of the Southern History Association* 8 (1904): 129–38.

Nicholson, Peter. *The Mechanics Companion*. New York: W. C. Borreadaile, 1831.

Oakleigh Period House Museum. Mobile: Historic Mobile Preservation Society, 1983.

O'Brien, Sean Michael. *Mobile, 1865: Last Stand of the Confederacy*. Westport, Conn.: Praeger, 2001.

Oldmixon, John W. *Transatlantic Wanderings*. London: Routledge, 1855.

Olmstead, Frederick Law. *The Cotton Kingdom: A Traveler's Observations on Cotton and Slavery in the American Slave States.* New York: Mason Brothers, 1861.

"Our Houses." *Harper's New Monthly Magazine* 19, no. 112 (September 1859): 513–18.

Owen, Thomas McAdory. *History of Alabama and Dictionary of Alabama Biography.* 4 vols. Chicago: S. J. Clarke Publishing, 1921.

Pierson, William H. *American Buildings and Their Architects: The Colonial and Neo-classical Styles.* New York: Anchor Books, 1976.

Pitts, J. R. S. *Life and Confession of the Noted Outlaw James Copeland.* 1858. Reprint, Jackson: University Press of Mississippi, 1980.

Riepma, Anne Sophie. *Fire and Fiction: Augusta Jane Evans in Context.* Amsterdam: Rodopi, 2000.

Rosenstiel, Helene von, and Gail Caskey Winkler. *Floor Coverings for Historic Buildings: A Guide to Selecting Reproductions.* Washington, D.C.: The Preservation Press, 1988.

Schumann, Ronnie. "'Cook's House' Exhibit Brings New Attention to Life Experiences of Oakleigh's Servant Class." *Landmark Letter* 39, no. 2 (Winter 2006): 2–3.

Scully, Arthur. *James Dakin, Architect: His Career in New York and the South.* Baton Rouge: Louisiana State University Press, 1973.

Sexton, Rebecca Grant. "The Letters of Augusta Evans Wilson, 1859–1906: Portrait of a Southern Patriot, Woman, and Writer." Dissertation, University of Georgia, 1999.

Shippee, Lester B., ed. *Bishop Whipple's Southern Diary, 1843-44.* New York: Da Capo Press, 1968.

Sledge, John S. "An Ornament to the City: Mobile's Government Street Presbyterian Church." *Gulf Coast Historical Review* 8, no. 2 (Spring 1993): 37–51.

Smith, J. Frazer. *White Pillars: The Architecture of the South.* New York: Bramhall House, 1941.

"Some Observations on Doors and Partitions." *Manufacturer and Builder* 3, no. 3 (March 1871): 62–63.

Stone, DeWitt Boyd, Jr., ed. *Wandering to Glory: Confederate Veterans Remember Evans' Brigade.* Columbia: University of South Carolina Press, 2002.

Thomason, Michael V. R., ed. *Mobile: The New History of Alabama's First City.* Tuscaloosa: University of Alabama Press, 2001.

Thompson, Alan Smith. "Mobile, Alabama, 1850–1861: Economic, Political, Physical, and Population Characteristics." Dissertation, University of Alabama, 1979.

Thompson, Rita K. *Building Mobile, Alabama: A Look at the Lives of Antebellum Tradesmen.* Mobile: Mobile Historic Development Commission, 2008.

Trollope, Frances. *Domestic Manners of the Americans.* 2 vols. London: Whittaker, Treacher and Co., 1832.

Turner, Suzanne, and J. J. Meek. *Gardens of Louisiana: Places of Work and Wonder.* Baton Rouge: Louisiana State University Press, 1997.

Van Rensselaer, Mrs. Schuyler. "Recent Architecture in America." *Century* 28, no. 1 (May 1884): 48–68.

Waselkov, Gregory A., and Bonnie L. Gums. *Plantation Archaeology at Riviere Aux Chiens, ca. 1725-1848.* Mobile: University of South Alabama, 2000.

Watson, Bama Wathan. *The History of Barton Academy.* Mobile: Haunted Book Shop, 1971.

Wiebenson, Dora. *Sources of Greek Revival Architecture.* London: A. Zwemmer, 1969.

Wilson, Charles Reagan, and William Ferris, eds. *Encyclopedia of Southern Culture.* Chapel Hill: University of North Carolina Press, 1989.

WEB SITES

Wallace, Frances Woolfolk. "Diary, March 19–August 25, 1864." Electronic edition online at www.docsouth.unc.edu/imls/wallace/menu.html

www.braggmitchellmansion.com

www.classicist.org/about

www.habitat.org/newsroom/2005archive/insitedoc008080.aspx

www.natchezpilgrimage.com

INDEX

Note: Italicized page numbers refer to photographs and their accompanying captions.

Acker, Marian Francis, 117, *118*
Adams, James J., 101
Alabama Catalog, The (Gamble), 2
Alabama Gulf Coast Art Colony, 118
Alabama Historical Commission, 122
Alabama Intelligencer and States Rights Expositor (newspaper), 16–17
Alabama Life Insurance and Trust Company, 60
Alabama Planter (newspaper), 101
Alabama Trust for Historic Preservation, 122
Alderson, William, 43, 70, 92–93, 94, 109, 112, 117
All in the Wrong (drama), 46
Allen, Ethan, 40
America (Smith), 2
American cottage. *See* Gulf Coast cottage
American Institute of Architects, 128n27
American Institution of Architects, 128n27
Andalusia, 8
Antiquities of Athens, The (Stuart and Revett), 3
Architect, The (Benjamin), 2, 11
Architecture in the United States, 1800–1850 (Maynard), 21, 23
Athens, Ga., 23
Azalea Trail, 118

Baldwin, Joseph G., 68
Bank of Mobile, 60
Bank of Pennsylvania, 5–6, 17, 23
Barnes, James, 49, 70, 74, 85, 86, 93, 112
Barton, Willoughby, 54
Barton Academy, *55*; Acker etching of, *118*; during Civil War, 111, 112; construction of, 54–56; design attribution of, 39, 48; on La Tourette map, 74, *74*; as public school, 131n22; restoration issues regarding, 121–23; rotunda of, *xxiv*, *57*, *58*; travelers' descriptions of, 75, 113
Baton Rouge, La., 16, 133n2
Beal, Gustavus, 66
Beal-Hunter House, 66–67, *67*
Beck, Mary Randelette, 118
Bell, Laura Spaulding, 43, *44*
Bellingrath Home, 127n4 (pref.)
Benjamin, Asher, 23, 63, 115; *The Architect*, 2, 11
Beroujon, Claude, 16, 28, 46, 61–62, 63, 92, 116
Beulah (Evans), x
Biddle, Nicholas, 6, 8, 60, 68, 69, 70
Bienville Square, 93
Bishop Portier House, 63–64, *64*
Black Belt, 46, 95, 108, 134n50
board of aldermen, 29
Board of School Commissioners, 54, 55, 56
bracketed Greek Revival, *4*, 108, *108*, 109, *110*
Bragg, Alexander J., 108, 134n50
Bragg, Judge John, 108, 109, 111
Bragg-Mitchell Mansion, *108*, 108–9, 120
Bremer, Fredrika, 94
brickyards, 45, 67, 82
Buckingham, J. S., 9, 75–76, 132n58
Builder's Guide, The (Hill), 41
Butt, Cary, 43, 70, 73, 74

C. B. Dakin and Brother, 47
Cahawba (boat), 101
Calef, Mary Jane, 100
Camp Beulah, 112
Captain Adams-Stone House, 100, 101, *102*
Carlen, Michael, 88, 89
Carlen House, 89, *89*, 100

Carmine Street Presbyterian Church, 15
Carolina Hall, ii, *90*, *91*, 91–92
carpenters' riot, 75
Cathedral, *57*, 61–62, *62*, 64, 92, 114, 121
Century (magazine), 19
Chestnut Street, 8
Choctaw (boat), 46
Choragic Monument of Lysicrates, 8, 53, 56
Christ Church (Episcopal), 50, 72, 73, 84, 85, 121; design and construction of, 70, 73, 92; 1840 illustration of, *71*
Church Street East Historic District, 56
City Hospital, 7, *31*, 36, 49, 73, 85, 115; design and construction of, 29–30, 32; on La Tourette Map, 74, *74*; during magazine explosion, 113; 1912 photograph of, *30*; restoration of, 121; traveler's description of, 113; U.S. Marine Hospital comparison with, 86
Clay, Henry, 84
Cleveland, U. T., 112
Collins, John K., 32, 49, 55, 77, 85; builds City Hospital, 29–30, 121; builds United States Hotel, 58, 68; lauds Hitchcock, 69
Colonial Dames, 86–87, 121
Comet (ship), 49
Conde-Charlotte House. *See* Jonathan Kirkbride House
Cooper, James Fenimore, 18
Copeland, James, 80–81
cottage, 159 S. Dearborn St., *116*
Creole cottage, 62–63, 64, 67, 131n31
Creole/Gulf Coast cottage. *See* Creole cottage; Gulf Coast cottage
Creoles, 84

Dakin, Charles, xii, 39, 73, 74; arrives in Mobile, 46; death of, 61,

82; marriage of, 50, 121; opens Mobile office, 40, 47–48; other activities of, 61; at Town and Davis, 16; works on Barton Academy, 55–56; works on Government Street Presbyterian Church, 49–50, 53; works on Planters and Merchants Bank, 59; works on United States Hotel, 58, 68

Dakin, James, 59, 83; arrives in Mobile, 40; death of, 133n2; designs Government Street Presbyterian Church interior, 53–54; designs United States Hotel, 58; drawing by, of St. Michael Street Hotel, *60*; founds American Institution of Architects, 128n27; shuttles between New Orleans and Mobile, 47; at Town and Davis, 15–16

Daugherty, Franklin, 122
Dauphin Street, 27, 41, 78, 80, 81, 88
Dauphin Way, 88
Davenport, Sarah Ann, 33
Davis, Alexander Jackson, 15, 43, 61
Davisean windows, 15, 50, 59, 70
Dawson, William, 88, 91
DeBow's Review, 16
Delbarco, Mary J., ix
Denniston, Harold Siebert ("Denny"), xxi, xxii, xxiii
Denniston, Lillian Pendaz, xxi
Denniston, Peggy, xxii
Denniston, Robert, *xx*, xxi, xxii, xxiii
Deshon, John J., 45
Dickens, Charles, 8
distyle in antis, 15, 50, 52, 61, 62, *62*, 70, 95

Eastern Shore, 76, 82, 100, 101, *102*
Economic Cottage Builder, The, 12
Ellis, Robert, 87
Ellison, Thomas, Jr., 43
Emanuel, Jonathon, 59, 60, 70, 109
Emanuel, Mary, 109
Emanuel House, xii, 59, 60, *61*, 116, *117*
Empire furniture, 12, 14, 127n4, 128n35
Erechtheum, 5

Erwin, Anna (Hitchcock), 40, 76, 130n36
Etchings of Old Mobile (Acker), 117–18, *118*
Evans, Augusta Jane, xii, xv, 35, 127n2; *Beulah*, x; *Inez*, x; *Macaria*, x; portrait of, *112*; *St. Elmo*, x
Everett, Mayor John, 30
Exploreum, 120
Eyes of the Storm, The (Hagler), xxii

Fairmount Waterworks, 6, 8
Faulkner, William, 20–21
Field, Anna, 101
Filmore, Millard, 101
fire, 14, 76, 87, 113; 1827 fire, 26–27, 36, 41, 78; 1839 fire, 78–81, *79*, 83; 1864 Courthouse fire, 112; Spring Hill College fire, 116
firemen, 79, 80, *96*, *97*
First Volunteer Regiment, 75
Flags in the Dust (*Sartoris*; Faulkner), 20, 129n57
Flush Times of Alabama and Mississippi, The (Baldwin), 68
Forks of Cypress, 16
Fort Morgan, 134n68
Franklin Institute, 6
Franklin Street Sabbath School Picnic, *94*
free blacks, 25, 42, 43, 83
From Builders to Architects (Gould), 2
From Fort to Port (Gould), 2

Gallier, James, Sr., xii, 41, 43, 47, 48; arrives in Mobile, 39, 40; on Barton Academy and Government Street Presbyterian Church, 48; Barton Academy design work of, 56; on Charles Dakin's death, 61; Christ Church alleged design role of, 70, 73; education of, 10–11; Government Street Presbyterian Church design role of, 49, 53; in New Orleans, 12, 44, 49; portrait of, *40*; at Town and Davis, 15–16
Gamble, Robert, 23; *The Alabama Catalog*, 2
Garfield, James, 35, 134n43

Georgia Cottage, *viii*, ix–xv, *xi*, *xiii*, 1, 88, 89; age of, 127n1; during Civil War, 112; as literary incubator, 127n2; painted, 118
Ghosts of Old Mobile (Beck), 118
Girard College, 8, 9, 84
Gone with the Wind (Mitchell), 21, 120
Goodman, Duke, 78
Gould, Elizabeth Barrett, 2
Government Street, xv, 48, 56, 59, 79, 85, 115; in Civil War, 111; travelers' descriptions of, 75, 94
Government Street Hotel. *See* United States Hotel
Government Street Presbyterian Church, xxi, xxvi, 51, *52*, *53*, 61; attic of, *18*; congregation of, in Civil War, 111; design and construction of, 39, 48–50, 52–54; interior of, *54*; on La Tourette Map, 74, *74*; as National Historic Landmark, 50; in twentieth century, 121; traveler's descriptions of, 75, 84
Gowans, Alan, 23
Graff, Frederick, 6
Greek Revival Architecture in America (Hamlin), 21
Greenberg, Allan, 23, 24
Gulf Coast cottage, *10*, *13*, 62–64, 89, *89*, 100, *103*, 115

Habitat for Humanity, 23
Hall, Edward, 64, 70
Hall, Mary Frances, 108
Hall-Ford House, xvi, 20, 63, 64, 65
Hamilton, Palmer C., 123, *123*
Hamilton, Peter Joseph, 109–11, 113; *A Little Boy in Confederate Mobile*, 109
Hamilton, Thomas, 27
Hamilton, Rev. William, 48, 49, 69, 76, 79, 84
Hamlin, Talbot, 23; *Greek Revival Architecture in America*, 21
Hamlin thesis, 21, 23, 129n61
Hardaway, William A., ix
Harpers New Monthly Magazine, 19

Harris, Joel Chandler, 19; *In Ole Virginia*, 20; *Nights with Uncle Remus*, 19
Henrietta at the Well (painting), xii
Henry Hitchcock Award, 132n64
Hill, Chester, 41
Historic American Buildings Survey, 103
Historic Mobile Preservation Society, 119, 121, 122
Hitchcock, Henry: background of, 40; bankruptcy of, 69–70; grave of, 77, 132n63; legacy of, 77–78; on Mobile's progress, 68–69; portrait of, *40*; role of, in building Barton Academy, 54–55; role of, in building Government Street Presbyterian Church, 48–50; role of, in building United States Hotel and Planters and Merchants Bank, 57–59; sickness and death of, 76–77; and Three Sisters, 65, 77
Hobart, Peter, 26, 27, 29, 45, 54
Hogan, J. B., 85
Holmes, Nicholas, Jr., *122*
Home as Found (Cooper), 18
Hone, Philip, 9
Hunley (submarine), 111

In Ole Virginia (Harris), 20
Inez (Evans), x

J. S. Kellogg and Co., 41
Jackson, Andrew, 8, 68
James, Laura Bell, *44*
James, Thomas S., 43–45; Bragg mansion attributed to, 109; builds Barton Academy, 55; builds Government Street Presbyterian Church, 49–50; builds Ottenstein House, 65, *66*; builds United States Hotel, 58; lauds Hitchcock, 69; portrait of, *44*; slave labor usage of, 45; throttled for Unionism, 111–12
Jefferson, Thomas, 5, 17
Jesuits, 28
Jonathan Kirkbride House, 86–88, *88*, 118, 121
Jonathon Emanuel House. *See* Emanuel House

Judson, Lewis, 26
Junior (ship), 101

Kearley, Douglas Burtu, 123, *123*
Kennedy, Joshua, Jr., 109
Kennedy House, 4, 109, *110*, 117
Kirkbride House. *See* Jonathan Kirkbride House
Koch, Albert C., 84

La Tourette, John, 74
La Tourette map (1838), 74, *74*
Lady Washington, 96
Lafever, Minard, xii, 11, 16, 53, 115
Lamb, Charles, xiv, 127n4
Latrobe, Benjamin Henry, 5–6, 8, 17, 63
lions of Philadelphia, 6, 9
Little Boy in Confederate Mobile, A (Peter Joseph Hamilton), 109
London Morning Post, 83
Louisiana and Alabama Diocese, 74
Lowery-Garner House, *10*
lumberyards, 45–46, 82, 95

Macaria (Evans), x
MacKenzie, Roderick, xii
magazine explosion, 113–14, 134nn68–69
Magnolia Hall, 17, 128n46
Manufacturer and Builder (journal), 14
Marengo County Directory, 43
Marine Street, 85, 123, *123*
Marshall, Benjamin Franklin, 103, 111
Marshall, Mrs., 103
Marshall-Dixon House, 101, 103, *106*, *107*, 123
Maynard, W. Barksdale, 21
McClure House, *119*
McCrary, David F., 17
McGehee, Tom, 127n4
Meaher, Augustine, III, xv
Mechanics Aid Association, 97
Mechanics House, 41
Mechanics Retreat, 41, *42*
Merchants and Planters Journal, 81
Merchants' Exchange, 8, 9
Mitchell, Alfred, 120

Mitchell, Margaret, 21; *Gone with the Wind*, 21, 120
Mitchell, Minnie, 120
Mobile Bay, 76, 100
Mobile Bay Monthly Magazine, 122
Mobile Carpentry and Joiners' Mutual Benefit Society, 42
Mobile Commercial Register (newspaper), 25, 70, 80
Mobile County Courthouse: 1825 building, 25–26, 27, 92; 1854 building, 92–93, 112; 1874 building, 134n62
Mobile County Department of Pensions and Securities, 121
Mobile County Health Department, 85–86, 121
Mobile Daily Register (newspaper), 92
Mobile Historic Development Commission, 122, 132n64
Mobile Hotel, 27
Mobile Register (newspaper), 38, 122
Monticello, 5
Moore, Lt. J. Wilkins, 113
Morris, William, III, 23
Murphy, Rev. Murdock, 48
Murphy High School, 89
Museum of Mobile, 131n10

Natchez, Miss., 16, 21
National Society of the Colonial Dames of America, 86–87, 121
New Englander and Yale Review, 19
New Orleans Daily Picayune (newspaper), 78, 83
New York Times (newspaper), 21
News Building, 23
Nichols, William, 16
Nights with Uncle Remus (Harris), 19
North American Review, 9
Nugent, John, 86

Oakleigh, *32*, *35*, *37*, *38*, 68, *120*; Bragg mansion compared with, 109; brickyard at, 45; construction of, 33; Denniston family at, xxi–xxiii, 118–19; description of, 35–36; floor plan of, *36*; historic

photograph of, *33*; staircase of, *xx*, *34*
O'Brien, Catherine, 60
Old Shell Road, 103
Oldmixon, John W., 9, 94
Olmstead, Frederick Law, 93
159 S. Dearborn Street cottage, 116
Ottenstein House, 65–66, *66*

Page, Thomas Nelson, 19–20
Palmer, Hebron, 43, 61, 117
Panic of 1837, 68
Parmly, Ludolph, 99
Parmly House, 97, *98*, 99
Parsons, Benjamin F., 17
Parthenon, 5, 6, 8, 17
Pentelique, 6
Philadelphia Courier (newspaper), 80
Phoenix No. 6, 79
pilastrades, 15, 50, 58, 61, 70
Places in Peril list, 122
Planters and Merchants Bank, 59, 68, 73, 79, *79*, 116, 133n2
Polk, Bishop Leonidas, 74
Portier, Bishop Michael: and Cathedral, 61–62, 68–69, 92; on magazine explosion, 114; personal residence of, 63–64; and Springhill College, 28
Presbytery of Alabama, 48
Psalm 37:37, 132n63

Ravesies, Frederick P., 99
Ravesies, Isabella, 99
Ravesies House, 97, 99, *99*
Rensselaer, Mrs. Schuyler Van, 19
Revett, Nicholas. *See* Stuart and Revett
Roberts, Joel, 100
Roberts, Mary, 97
Roberts-Abbot House, 97, *97*, 109
Roberts-Staples House, 100, *100*
Roper, James W., xxiii, 32–33, 35, 68; portrait of, *32*
Roper Street, xxii
Royal Street, 79, 83
Russell, Melissa, 39

Sartoris (Faulkner), 20, 129n57
Sartoris, John, 20

sawmills, 45, 67, 82
School of Fine Arts (Dublin), 10
Schuylkill River, 6
Seale William, 109
Second Bank of the United States, 8, 9, 60, 68
Signor Vito Viti & Sons, 95
slaves, 17, 21, 25, 83; as artisans, 42–43, 45; at Carolina Hall, 91–92; and 1839 fire, 80; Roper's, 33, 36, 68; yellow fever deaths of, 132n61
Sledge, Edward Simmons, x
Sledge, Mary Frank Sturdivant, x
Smith, Samuel F., 1–2; *America*, 2
So Red the Rose (Stark Young), 21
Society of Dilettanti, 3
Sousa, John Philip, xxiii
Southerland, Genevieve, 118
Southern Market/City Hall, 131n10
Spanish Fort, 11, 113
Sprigs of Laurel (drama), 46
Spring Hill, 76, 82, 88, *90*, 91, 101
Spring Hill Avenue, xi, xv, 38, 88, 108
Spring Hill College, 28, 29, 103, 116
Spring Hill Road, ix, 88
St. Anthony Street, 30, 73
St. Charles Hotel (New Orleans), 12, 44, 49
St. Elmo (Evans), x
St. John (ship), 49
St. Michael Street Hotel, 59, *60*
Stewart, Roger, 101
Stewartfield, 101, *102*, 103, *103*, *104*, *105*
Strickland, William, 8
Stuart, James ("Athenian"). *See* Stuart and Revett
Stuart and Revett, 5, 6, 8, 127n4 (intro.); *The Antiquities of Athens*, 3
Summerville, 108

Tardy Cottage, *13*
Temple of Minerva. *See* Parthenon
Temple of Theseus, 5
Tennessee (ship), 111
Three Sisters, 77
Tombigbee River, 83
Toombs, Robert, xiv

Tower of the Winds, 5, 91
Town, Ithiel, 15
Town and Davis, 15–16, 50, 53, 70, 73
tradesmen, 11–12, 42, *42*, 44, 75, 95
Trollope, Anthony, 8
Trollope, Fanny, 8, 14
Twentieth Iowa Division (U.S. Army), 113

Unitarian Church, 61
United States Bank, 6
United States Hotel, 58, 68, 75, 79, 83; on La Tourette Map, 74, *74*
University of Miami, 23
University of Notre Dame, 23
University of Virginia, 5
U.S. Marine Hospital, 73, *85*, 85–86, 113, 117, 121

Virginia state house, 5

Wallace, Frances Woolfolk, 113
Wallace, Gov. George C., 122
Walpole, Horace, 5
Walter, Thomas U., 8, 18, 128n27
Waring, Moses, 86
Waring-Texas House, 22, 86, *87*
Washington Number 8 (renamed 5), *96*, 96–97
Washington Street Methodist Episcopal Church, 50
Waverly, 95
Webb, Caroline, 50
Webster, Daniel, 111
Whipple, Henry, 9, 84
Williamson, Robert, 85
Wills, Rev. William H., 83
Wilson, Augusta Evans. *See* Evans, Augusta Jane
Wilson, Col. Lorenzo, xii
Wilson, Samuel, Jr., 87

yellow fever, 39, 61, 81, 82, 101; death figures in 1839, 132nn60–61; epidemic of 1839, 76; Hitchcock succumbs to, 76
Young, Col. George H., 95
Young, Stark, 21